When you were dead in your sins
and in the uncircumcision of
your sinful nature, God made
you aliv[e] [...] forgave
us all o[...] [...]nceled
the writt[en] [...]
regulations, that was against
us and that stood opposed to us;
he took it away, nailing it to the
cross. ~Colossians 2:13-14

POWER
in the
BLOOD

POWER
in the
BLOOD

Charles Spurgeon

Whitaker House

All Scripture quotations are taken from the *King James Version* (KJV) of the Bible.

POWER IN THE BLOOD

ISBN: 0-88368-427-6
Printed in the United States of America
Copyright © 1996 by Whitaker House

Whitaker House
30 Hunt Valley Circle
New Kensington, PA 15068

3 4 5 6 7 8 9 10 11 12 13 / 06 05 04 03 02 01 00 99

Contents

1

Healing by the Stripes of Jesus

With his stripes we are healed.
—Isaiah 53:5

One evening in Exeter Hall, I heard a speech by the late Mr. Mackay. He told of a person who was very concerned about his soul and felt that he could never rest until he found salvation. So, taking the Bible in his hand, he said to himself, "Eternal life is to be found somewhere in the Word of God; and if it is here, I will find it, for I will read the Book right through. I will pray to God over every page of it. Possibly, it may contain some saving message for me."

He told us that the earnest seeker read on through Genesis, Exodus, Leviticus, and so on; and though Christ is there very evidently, he could not find Him in the types and symbols.

The holy histories did not yield him comfort, nor did the book of Job. He passed through Psalms but did not find his Savior there, and the same was the case with the other books, until he reached Isaiah. In this book he read on until near the end, and then in the fifty-third chapter these words arrested his delighted attention: "With his stripes we are healed" (v. 5).

"Now I have found it," he said. "Here is the healing that I need for my sin-sick soul, and I see how it comes to me through the sufferings of the Lord Jesus Christ. Blessed be His name, I am healed!" It was well that the seeker was wise enough to search the Sacred Volume; it was better still that in that volume there was a life-giving word that the Holy Spirit revealed to the seeker's heart.

I have decided that Isaiah 53:5 is a fine text on which to write. Perhaps a voice from God may speak through it yet again to some other awakened sinner. By this verse God spoke to the treasurer of the Ethiopian queen; he was impressed by it while searching the Scriptures. (See Acts 8:26–38.) May God also speak to many who will read this book! Let us pray that it may be so. God is very gracious, and He will hear our prayers.

The object of this chapter is very simple: I want to explain my text, Isaiah 53:5. May the Holy Spirit give me power to do so to the glory of God!

The Disease of Sin

In endeavoring to explain the full meaning of the text, I would remark first that God, in His infinite mercy, here treats sin as a disease. "With his stripes"—that is, the stripes of the Lord Jesus—"we are healed" (Isa. 53:5). Through the sufferings of our Lord, sin is pardoned, and we are delivered from the power of evil. We are healed of the deadly malady of sin.

In this present life, the Lord treats sin as a disease. If He were to treat it at once as sin and summon us to His court to answer for it, we would immediately sink beyond the reach of hope, for we could neither answer His accusations nor defend ourselves from His justice. In His great mercy He looks upon us with pity, and for now He treats our ill manners as if they were diseases to be cured rather than rebellions to be punished.

It is most gracious on His part to do so, for while sin is a disease, it is also a great deal more. If our iniquities were the result of an unavoidable sickness, we might claim pity rather than scolding. However, we sin willfully; we choose evil; we transgress in heart. Therefore, we bear a moral responsibility that

9

makes sin an infinite evil. Our sin is our crime rather than our calamity.

However, God looks at our sin as a disease for a season. So that He can deal with us on hopeful grounds, He looks at the sickness of sin and does not look yet at the wickedness of sin. This is not without reason, for men who indulge in gross vices are often charitably judged by their fellowmen to be not only wholly wicked, but partly mad. Propensities to evil are usually associated with some degree of mental disease and, perhaps, also, of physical disease. At any rate, sin is a spiritual malady of the worst kind.

The Abnormality of Sin

Sin is a disease, for it is neither essential to manhood nor an integral part of human nature as God created it. Man was never more fully and truly man than he was before he fell. He who is specially called "the Son of man" (Matt. 8:20) "did no sin, neither was guile found in his mouth" (1 Pet. 2:22), yet He was perfectly man.

Sin is abnormal, a sort of cancerous growth that should not be in the soul. Sin is disturbing to manhood: sin unmans a man. Sin is sadly destructive to man; it takes the crown from his head, the light from his mind, and the joy from his heart. We may name many grievous diseases that are destroyers of our race, but the greatest of these is sin. Sin, indeed, is the fatal egg from which all other sicknesses have been hatched. It is the fountain and source of all mortal maladies.

The Disorder of Sin

Sin is a disease because it puts the whole system of the man out of order. It places the lower faculties in the higher place, for it makes the body master over the soul. The man should ride the horse, but in the sinner the horse rides the man. The mind should keep the animal instincts and propensities in check, but in many men the animal crushes the mental and the spiritual. For instance, how many live as if eating and drinking were the chief objects of existence; they live to eat, instead of eating to live!

The faculties are thrown out of gear by sin, so that they act fitfully and irregularly; you cannot depend on any one of them to keep its place. The equilibrium of the life forces is grievously disturbed. Even as a sickness of the body is called a disorder, so sin is the disorder of the soul. Human nature is out of joint and out of health, and man is no longer man. He is dead through sin (Eph. 2:1), even as he was warned of old, "In the day that thou eatest thereof thou shalt surely die" (Gen. 2:17). Man is marred, bruised, sick, paralyzed, polluted, and rotten with disease, just in proportion as sin has shown its true character.

The Undermining Nature of Sin

Sin, like disease, weakens man. The moral energy is so broken down in some people that it scarcely exists. The conscience labors under a fatal disease and is gradually ruined by a decline. The understanding has been lamed by evil, and the will is rendered feeble for good, though forcible for evil. The principle of integrity, the resolve of virtue—in which a man's true strength really lies—is sapped and undermined by wrongdoing.

Sin is like a secret bleeding that robs the vital parts of their essential nourishment. How near to death in some people is even the power to discern between good and evil! The apostle tells us that "when we were yet without strength, in due time Christ died for the ungodly" (Rom. 5:6). This being without strength is the direct result of the sickness of sin, which has weakened our whole manhood.

The Numbing Nature of Sin

Sin is a disease that in some cases causes extreme pain and anguish, but in other cases deadens sensibility. It frequently happens that the more sinful a man is, the less he is conscious of it.

It was remarked of a certain notorious criminal that many thought him innocent because when he was charged with murder, he did not betray the least emotion. In that wretched self-possession there was, to my mind, presumptive proof of his great familiarity with crime. If an innocent person is charged with a great offense, the mere charge horrifies him. It is only by weighing all the circumstances and distinguishing between sin and shame that he recovers himself. It is he who can do the deed of shame that does not blush when he is charged with it.

The deeper a man goes into sin, the less he concedes that it is sin. Like a man who takes drugs, he acquires the power to take larger and larger doses, until that which would kill a hundred other men has only a slight effect on him. A man who readily lies is scarcely conscious of the moral degradation involved in being a liar, though he may think it shameful to be called one. It is one of the worst points of this disease of sin that it stupefies the understanding and causes a paralysis of the conscience.

By and by, sin is sure to cause pain, like other diseases that flesh is heir to; and when awakening comes, what a start it gives!

Conscience one day will awake and fill the guilty soul with alarm and distress, if not in this world, yet certainly in the next. Then the sinner will see what an awful thing it is to offend against the law of the Lord.

The Impurity of Sin

Sin is a disease that pollutes a man. Certain diseases render a man horribly impure. God is the best judge of purity, for He is exceedingly holy and cannot endure sin. The Lord puts sin from Him with abhorrence, and He prepares a place where the forever unclean will be shut up by themselves. He will not dwell with them here, nor can they dwell with Him in heaven. As men must put lepers apart by themselves, so justice must put out of heaven everything that defiles. Oh, my reader, will the Lord be compelled to put you out of His presence because you persist in wickedness?

The disease of sin, which is so polluting, is, at the same time, most injurious to us, for it prevents the higher enjoyment and employment of life. People can exist in sin, but they do not truly live. As the Scripture says, such a person is "dead while [he] liveth" (1 Tim. 5:6). While we continue in sin, we cannot serve God on earth or hope to enjoy Him forever above.

We are incapable of communion with perfect spirits and with God Himself, and the loss of this communion is the greatest of all evils. Sin deprives us of spiritual sight, hearing, feeling, and taste, and thus deprives us of those joys that turn existence into life. It brings true death upon us, so that we exist in ruins, deprived of all that can be called life.

The Fatality of Sin

This disease is also fatal. Is it not written, "The soul that sinneth, it shall die" (Ezek. 18:4)? "Sin, when it is finished, bringeth forth death" (James 1:15). There is no hope of eternal life for any man unless sin is put away. This disease never exhausts itself or destroys itself. "Evil men...wax worse and worse" (2 Tim. 3:13). In another world, as well as in this present world, character will go on to develop and ripen, and so the sinner will become more and more corrupt as the result of his spiritual death.

Oh, my friends, if you refuse Christ, sin will be the death of your peace, your joy, your prospects, your hopes, and thus the death of all that is worth having! In the case of other diseases, nature may conquer the malady, and you may be restored; but in this case, apart from divine intervention, nothing lies before you but eternal death.

God, therefore, treats sin as a disease because it is a disease. And I want you to believe that it is so, for then you will thank the Lord for treating your sin this way. Many of us have felt that sin is a disease and have been healed of it. Oh, that others could see what an exceedingly evil thing it is to sin against the Lord! It is a contagious, defiling, incurable, mortal sickness.

Perhaps somebody is saying, "Why do you raise these points? They fill us with unpleasant thoughts." I do it for the reason given by the engineer who built the great Menai Tubular Bridge. When it was being erected, some engineer friends said to him, "You raise all kinds of difficulties."

"Yes," he said, "I raise them so that I may solve them."

That is why I expound on the sad state of man, so that I may present the glorious remedy of which our text so sweetly speaks.

THE REMEDY FOR SIN

God treats sin as a disease, and He here declares the remedy that He has provided: "With his stripes we are healed" (Isa. 53:5). I ask you very solemnly to accompany me in your meditations for a few minutes, while I bring before you the stripes of the Lord Jesus.

The Lord resolved to restore us, and therefore He sent His only begotten Son (John 3:16), very God of very God. God's Son descended into this world to take upon Himself our nature (Heb. 2:16) in order to redeem us. He lived as a man among men (Phil. 2:8); and, in due time, after thirty years or more of service, the time came when He should do us the greatest service of all. Namely, He stood in our stead and bore "the chastisement of our peace" (Isa. 53:5). He went to Gethsemane, and there, at the first taste of our bitter cup, He sweat great drops of blood (Luke 22:44). He went to Pilate's hall and Herod's judgment seat, and there He suffered a great deal of pain and scorn in our place. Last of all, they took Him to the cross and nailed Him there to die—to die in our stead—"the just for the unjust, that he might bring us to God" (1 Pet. 3:18).

The word *stripes* is used to set forth His sufferings, both of body and of soul. The whole of Christ was made a sacrifice for us: His whole manhood suffered. His body and His mind shared in a grief that can never be fully described. In the beginning of His passion, when He emphatically suffered instead of us, He was in agony, and from His body a bloody sweat flowed so heavily that it fell to the ground (Luke 22:44). It is very rare for a man to sweat blood. There have been one or two instances of

it, and they have been followed by almost immediate death. But our Savior lived—lived after an agony that, to anyone else, would have proved fatal.

Before He could cleanse His face from this dreadful crimson, they hurried Him to the high priest's hall. In the dead of night they bound Him and led Him away. Then they took Him to Pilate and to Herod. They scourged Him (Matt. 27:26), and their soldiers spat on Him and struck Him (Matt. 27:30) and put on His head a crown of thorns (Matt. 27:29).

Scourging is one of the most awful tortures that can be inflicted. It is to the eternal disgrace of Englishmen that they permitted the cat-o'-nine-tails to be used on the soldier; but to the Romans, cruelty was so natural that they made their common punishments worse than brutal. The Roman scourge is said to have been made of the sinews of oxen, twisted into knots, and into these knots were inserted both slivers of bone and the hipbones of sheep. Every time the scourge fell upon the bare back, "the plowers...made long their furrows" (Ps. 129:3). Our Savior was called upon to endure the fierce pain of the Roman scourge, and this not as the end of His punishment, but as a preliminary to crucifixion.

In addition to this, they struck Him and plucked out His hair; they spared Him no form

of pain. In all His faintness, through bleeding and fasting, they made Him carry His cross (John 19:17). Then another was forced, by the forethought of their cruelty, to bear the cross (Matt. 27:32), lest their victim should die on the road. They stripped Him and threw Him down and nailed Him to the wood. They pierced His hands and His feet (Ps. 22:16). They lifted up the cross with Him on it, and then they dashed it down into its place in the ground, so that all His limbs were dislocated. This was done in accordance with Psalm 22:14: "I am poured out like water, and all my bones are out of joint." He hung in the burning sun until the fever dissolved His strength, and He said,

> *My heart is like wax; it is melted in the*
> *midst of my bowels. My strength is dried*
> *up like a potsherd; and my tongue*
> *cleaveth to my jaws; and thou hast*
> *brought me into the dust of death.*
> *(Ps. 22:14–15)*

There He hung, in the sight of God and men.

The weight of His body was first sustained by His feet, until the nails tore through the tender nerves; and then the painful load began to weigh on His hands and tear that sensitive flesh. How small a wound in the hand has brought on lockjaw! How awful must have been the torment caused by that dragging iron tearing through the delicate parts of the hands and feet! Now every kind of bodily pain tortured His body.

All the while His enemies stood around, pointing at Him in scorn, sticking out their tongues in mockery, scoffing at His prayers, and gloating over His sufferings. He cried, "I thirst" (John 19:28), and they gave Him vinegar "mingled with gall" (Matt. 27:34). After a while He said, "It is finished" (John 19:30). He had endured the utmost of appointed grief and had made full vindication to divine justice. Then, and not until then, He "gave up the ghost" (John 19:30).

Holy men of old have expounded most lovingly on the bodily sufferings of our Lord, and I have no hesitation in doing the same. I trust that trembling sinners may see salvation in these painful stripes of the Redeemer.

To describe the outward sufferings of our Lord is not easy: I acknowledge that I have failed. But His soul sufferings, which were the soul of His sufferings, who can even conceive, much less express? At the very first I told you that He sweat great drops of blood (Luke 22:44). That was His heart driving out its life to the surface because of His terrible depression of spirit. He said, "My soul is exceeding sorrowful, even unto death" (Matt. 26:38). The betrayal by Judas (Matt. 26:47–49) and the desertion of the Twelve (Matt. 26:56) grieved our Lord, but the weight of our sin was the real pressure on His heart. Our guilt was the olive press that forced from Him the moisture of His life.

No language can ever tell His agony in the prospect of His passion; how little then can we comprehend the passion itself? When nailed to the cross, He endured what no martyr ever suffered; for martyrs, when they have died, have been so sustained by God that they have rejoiced amid their pain. But, our Redeemer was forsaken by His Father, and He cried, "My God, my God, why hast thou forsaken me?" (Ps. 22:1). That was the bitterest cry of all, the utmost depth of His unfathomable grief. Yet, it was necessary for Christ to be deserted because God must turn His back on sin, and consequently on Him who was made "to be sin for us" (2 Cor. 5:21).

The soul of the great Substitute suffered a horror of misery so that sinners would not have to experience the horror of hell. We would have been plunged into hell, but Jesus took our sin upon Himself and was "made a curse for us: for it is written, Cursed is every one that hangeth on a tree" (Gal. 3:13). But who can comprehend what that curse means?

The remedy for your sins and mine is found in the substitutionary sufferings of the Lord Jesus, and in these alone. These stripes of the Lord Jesus Christ were on our behalf. Do you ask, "Is there anything for us to do to remove the guilt of sin?" I answer: There is nothing whatsoever for you to do. By the stripes of Jesus we are healed. All those stripes He has endured, and He has not left one of them for us to bear.

"But do we not have to believe on Him?" Yes, certainly. If I claim that a certain ointment heals, I do not deny that you need a bandage with which to apply it to the wound. Faith is the bandage that binds the ointment of Christ's reconciliation to the sore of our sin. The bandage does not heal; that is the work of the ointment. Likewise, faith does not heal; that is the work of the atonement of Christ.

Do I hear someone say, "But surely I must do something or suffer something"? I answer: You must not try to add anything to Christ's atonement, or you greatly dishonor Him. For your salvation, you must rely on the wounds of Jesus Christ and nothing else. The text does not say, "His stripes help to heal us," but, "With his stripes we are healed" (Isa. 53:5).

"But we must repent," cries another. Assuredly we must, and will, for repentance is the first sign of healing; but the stripes of Jesus heal us, not our repentance. These stripes, when applied to the heart, work repentance in us: we hate sin because it made Jesus suffer.

When you believe that Jesus suffered for you, then you discover the fact that God will never punish you for the same offense for which Jesus died. His justice will not permit Him to see the debt paid first by the surety, and then again by the debtor. Justice cannot demand a recompense twice; if my bleeding Substitute has borne my guilt, then I cannot bear it. Accepting Christ Jesus as having suffered for me, I have accepted a complete discharge from judicial liability. I have been condemned in Christ, and there is, therefore, now no condemnation to me anymore (Rom. 8:1).

This is the groundwork of the security of the sinner who believes in Jesus. He lives because Jesus died in his place, and he is acceptable before God because Jesus is accepted. The person for whom Jesus is an accepted Substitute must go free. None can touch him; he is clear. Oh, my reader, will you take Jesus Christ as your Substitute? If so, you are free. "He that believeth on him is not condemned" (John 3:18). Thus, "with his stripes we are healed" (Isa. 53:5).

THE POWER OF THIS REMEDY

I have tried to put before you the disease and the remedy. I now desire to explain the fact that this remedy is effective immediately wherever it is applied. The stripes of Jesus do heal men; they have healed many of us. It does not look as if they could cause so great a cure, but the fact is undeniable.

I often hear people say, "If you preach this faith in Jesus Christ as the means of salvation, people will be careless about holy living." I am as good a witness on that point as anybody, for I live every day in the midst of men who are trusting in the stripes of Jesus for their salvation. I have seen no bad effect from such a trust, but I have seen the reverse. I bear testimony that I have seen the very worst of men become the very best of men by believing in the Lord Jesus Christ. It is surprising how these stripes heal the moral diseases of those who seem past remedy.

I have seen a sinner's character healed. I have seen the drunkard become sober, the harlot become chaste, the angry man become gentle, the covetous man become generous, and the liar become truthful, simply by trusting in the sufferings of Jesus. If trusting in Jesus did not make a person righteous, it would not really do anything for him. You must judge a person by his fruits (Matt. 7:20). If the fruits are not changed, the tree is not changed. Character is everything; if the character is not set right, the person is not saved.

I say without fear of contradiction that the atoning sacrifice, applied to the heart, heals the disease of sin. If you doubt it, try it. He who believes in Jesus is sanctified (Heb. 10:10) as well as justified (Rom. 3:24); by faith he becomes an altogether changed person.

Not only is the character healed, but the conscience is healed of its sting. Sin crushes a person's soul; he is spiritless and joyless. But the moment he believes in Jesus, he leaps into the light. You can often see a change even in the person's face; the cloud flies from the countenance when guilt goes from the conscience. Dozens of times, when I have been talking with those bowed down with sin's burden, they have looked as though they qualified for an asylum because of their inward grief. But they have caught the thought, "Christ stood for me; and if I trust in Him, I have the sign that He did so, and I am clear," and their faces have lit up as if they had glimpsed heaven.

Gratitude for such great mercy causes a change of thought towards God, and so it heals the judgment. By this means, the affections are turned in the right way, and the heart is healed. Sin is no longer loved, but God is loved, and holiness is desired. The whole man is healed, and the whole life is changed. How lighthearted a person is made by faith in Jesus! How the troubles of life lose their weight! How the fear of death is gone! A convert rejoices in the Lord, for the blessed remedy of the stripes of Jesus is applied to his soul by faith in Him.

The fact that "with his stripes we are healed" (Isa. 53:5) has plenty of evidence. I will take the liberty of giving my own testimony. If it were necessary, I could call thousands of people, my daily acquaintances, who can say that with the stripes of Christ they are healed. Even so, I must not withhold my personal testimony. Suppose I had suffered from a dreadful disease and a physician had given me a remedy that had healed me. I would not be ashamed to tell you all about it. I would use my own case as an argument to persuade you to use my physician.

Years ago, when I was a youth, the burden of my sin was exceedingly heavy upon me. I had not fallen into any great sins, and I was not regarded by anyone as an especially evil transgressor. However, I regarded myself as such, and I had good reason for doing so. My conscience was sensitive because it was enlightened; and I judged that, having a godly father and a praying mother, and having been trained in the ways of piety, I had sinned against much light. Consequently, there was a greater degree of guilt in my sin than in that of others who were my youthful associates, who had not enjoyed my advantages.

I could not enjoy the fun of youth because I felt that I had damaged my conscience. I would go to my room and there sit alone, read my Bible, and pray for forgiveness, but peace did not come to me. Books such as Baxter's *Call to the Unconverted* and Doddridge's *Rise and Progress* I read over and over again. Early in the morning I would awake and read the most earnest religious books I could find, desiring to be eased of my burden of sin. I was not always this dull, but at times my misery of soul was very great. The words of the weeping prophet and of Job suited my mournful case. I would have chosen death rather than life. I tried to do as well as I could and behave myself, but in my own judgment I grew worse and worse. I felt more and more despondent.

I attended every place of worship within my reach, but I heard nothing that gave me lasting comfort. Finally, one day I heard a simple preacher of the Gospel speak from the text, "Look unto me, and be ye saved, all the ends of the earth" (Isa. 45:22). When he told me that all I had to do was look to Jesus—to Jesus the Crucified One—I could scarcely believe it. He went on and said, "Look, look, look!" He added, "There is a young man, under the left-hand gallery there, who is very miserable. He will have no peace until he looks to Jesus." Then he cried, "Look! Look! Young man, look!" I did look. In that moment relief came to me, and I felt such overflowing joy that I could have stood up and cried, "Hallelujah! Glory be to God! I am delivered from the burden of my sin!"

Many days have passed since then, but my faith has held me up and compelled me to tell the story of free grace and dying love. I can truly say,

> E'er since by faith I saw the stream
> Thy flowing wounds supply,
> Redeeming love has been my theme,
> And shall be till I die.

I hope to sit up in bed during my last hours and tell of the stripes that healed me. I hope some young men, yes, and old men, will at once try this remedy. It is good for all characters and all ages. "With his stripes we are healed" (Isa. 53:5). Thousands upon thousands of us have tried and proven this remedy. "We speak that we do know, and testify that we have seen" (John 3:11). God grant that others may receive our witness through the power of the Holy Spirit!

I want to write a few lines to those who have not tried this marvelous cure. Let my words speak directly to you. Friend, you are by nature in need of soul healing as much as anybody, and one reason that you do not care about the remedy is that you do not believe you are sick. I saw a salesman one day as I was taking a walk; he was selling walking sticks. He followed me and offered me one of the sticks. I showed him mine—a far better one than any he had to sell—and he left at once. He could see that I was not likely to be a purchaser.

I have often thought of that when I have been preaching. I show men the righteousness of the Lord Jesus, but they show me their own, and all hope of dealing with them is gone. Unless I can show them that their righteousness is worthless, they will not seek "the righteousness which is of God by faith" (Phil. 3:9). Oh, that the Lord would show you your disease, and then you would desire the remedy!

It may be that you do not care to hear of the Lord Jesus Christ. Ah, my dear friends! You will have to hear of Him one of these days, either for your salvation or your condemnation. The Lord has the key to your heart, and I trust He will give you a better mind. Then, your memory will recall my simple words, and you will say, "I do remember. Yes, I read that there is healing in the wounds of Christ."

I pray you do not put off seeking the Lord; that would be great presumption on your part and a sad provocation to Him. But, if you have put it off, I pray you do not let the Devil tell you it is too late. It is never too late while life lasts. I have read in books that very few people are converted after forty years of age. I am solemnly convinced that there is little truth in such a statement. I have seen as many people converted at one age as at another in proportion to the number of people who are living at that age. Any first Sunday in the month there are thirty to eighty new converts in our church who are given the right hand of fellowship. This selection of people represents every age, from childhood up to old age.

The precious blood of Jesus has power to heal long-rooted sin. It makes old hearts new. If you were a thousand years old, I would exhort you to believe in Jesus, and I would be sure that His stripes would heal you. Your hair is nearly gone, old friend, and wrinkles appear on your brow, but come to Jesus now! You are rotting away with sin, but this medicine heals desperate cases! Retiree, put your trust in Jesus, for with His stripes the old and the dying are healed!

Now, my dear friend, you are at this moment either healed or not. You are either healed by grace, or you are still in your natural sickness. Will you be so kind to yourself as to inquire which it is? Many say, "We know what we are"; but some more thoughtful ones reply, "We don't quite know." Friend, you ought to know. Suppose I asked a man, "Are you bankrupt or not?" and he said, "I really have no time to look at my books, and therefore I am not sure." I would suspect that he was in financial trouble; would not you? Whenever a man is afraid to look at his books, I suspect that he has something to be afraid of. So, whenever a person says, "I don't know my condition, and I don't care to think much about it," you may pretty safely conclude that things are not right between him and God. You ought to know whether you are saved or not.

"I hope I am saved," says one, "but I do not know the date of my conversion." That does not matter at all. It is a pleasant thing for a person to know his birthday; but when a person is not sure of the exact date of his birth, he does not, therefore, infer that he is not alive! If a person does not know when he was converted, that is no proof that he is not converted.

The point is, do you trust Jesus Christ? Has that trust made a new person out of you? Has your confidence in Christ made you feel that you have been forgiven? Do you love God for forgiving you, and has that love become the mainspring of your being, so that out of love to God you delight to obey Him? Then you are healed. If you do not believe in Jesus, be sure that you are still not healed, and I pray you look at my text until you are led by grace to say, "I am healed, for I have trusted in the stripes of Jesus."

Suppose, for a moment, you are not healed; let me ask the question, "Why aren't you?" You know the Gospel; why are you not healed by Christ? "I don't know," says one. But, my dear friend, I entreat you not to rest until you do know.

"I can't find the way," says another. The other day a young girl was putting a button on her father's coat. She was sitting with her back to the window, and she said, "Father, I can't see. I am blocking my own light."

He replied, "Ah, my daughter, that is what you have been doing all your life!"

This is the position of some of you spiritually. You are blocking your own light; you think too much of yourselves. There is plenty of light in the Sun of Righteousness, but you get in the dark by putting self in the way of that Sun. Oh, that your self might be put away!

I read a touching story the other day about how one young man found peace. For some time he had been under conviction of sin, longing to find mercy, but he could not reach it. He was a telegraph clerk, and being in the office one morning, he had to receive and transmit a telegram. To his great surprise, he spelled out these words: "Behold the Lamb of God, which taketh away the sin of the world" (John 1:29). A gentleman on vacation was telegraphing a message to a friend whose soul was in distress. The message was meant for another, but he who transmitted it received eternal life as the words came flashing into his soul.

Oh, dear friends, get out of your own light, and at once "behold the Lamb of God, which taketh away the sin of the world"! I cannot telegraph the words to you, but I want to put them before you so plainly and distinctly that every troubled soul may know that they are meant for him. There lies your hope—not in yourself, but in the Lamb of God. Behold Him. And as you behold Him, your sin will be put away, and by His stripes you will be healed.

WORDS TO THE HEALED

If, dear friend, you are healed, this is my word to you: then get out of diseased company. Come away from the companions that have infected you with sin. "Come out from among them, and be ye separate, saith the Lord, and touch not the unclean thing" (2 Cor. 6:17).

If you are healed, praise the Healer, and acknowledge what He has done for you. There were ten lepers healed, but only one returned to praise the healing hand. Do not be among the ungrateful nine. (See Luke 17:12–19.)

If you have found Christ, confess His name. Confess it in His own appointed way: "He that believeth and is baptized shall be saved" (Mark 16:16). When you have thus confessed Him, speak out for Him. Tell what Jesus has done for your soul, and dedicate yourself to the holy purpose of spreading abroad the message by which you have been healed.

I had an experience related to me that pleased me. It shows how one man, being healed, may be the means of blessing to another. Many years ago I preached a sermon in Exeter Hall that was printed and entitled, "Salvation to the Uttermost." A friend, who lives not very far from me, was in the city of Para in Brazil. Here he heard of an Englishman in prison who had, in a state of drunkenness, committed a murder for which he was confined for life. My friend went to see him and found him deeply penitent, but quietly restful and happy in the Lord. He had felt the terrible wound of bloodguiltiness in his soul, but it had been healed, and he felt the bliss of pardon. Here is the story of the poor man's conversion in his own words:

Healing by the Stripes of Jesus

A young man, who had just completed his contract with the gasworks, was returning to England, but before doing so he called to see me, and brought with him a parcel of books. When I opened it, I found that they were novels; but, being able to read, I was thankful for anything. After I had read several of the books, I found a sermon (No. 84), preached by C. H. Spurgeon, in Exeter Hall, on June 8th, 1856, from the words, "Wherefore he is able also to save them to the uttermost" (Heb. 7:25). In his discourse, Mr. Spurgeon referred to Palmer, who was then lying under sentence of death in Stafford Goal, and in order to bring home this text to his hearers, he said that if Palmer had committed many other murders, if he repents and seeks God's pardoning love in Christ, even he will be forgiven! I then felt that if Palmer could be forgiven, so might I. I sought, and blessed be God, I found. I am pardoned, I am free; I am a sinner saved by grace. Though a murderer, I have not yet sinned "beyond the uttermost." Blessed be his holy name!

It made me very happy to think that a poor condemned murderer could thus be converted.

Surely, there is hope for every reader of this book, however guilty he may be!

If you know Christ, tell others about Him. You do not know what good there is in making Jesus known, even if all you can do is give a tract or repeat a verse. Dr. Valpy, the author of a great many books, wrote the following simple lines as his confession of faith:

> In peace let me resign my breath,
>   And thy salvation see;
> My sins deserve eternal death,
>   But Jesus died for me.

Valpy is dead and gone, but he gave those lines to dear old Dr. Marsh, the rector of Beckenham, who put them over his study mantelshelf. The earl of Roden came in and read them. "Will you give me a copy of those lines?" asked the good earl.

"I will be glad to," said Dr. Marsh, and he copied them. Lord Roden took them home and put them over *his* mantelshelf. General Taylor, a Waterloo hero, came into the room and noticed them. He read them over and over again while staying with Earl Roden, until his lordship remarked, "I say, friend Taylor, I should think you know those lines by heart."

He answered, "I do know them by heart; indeed, my very heart has grasped their meaning." He was brought to Christ by that humble rhyme.

General Taylor handed those lines to an officer in the army, who was going out to the Crimean war. He came home to die; and when Dr. Marsh went to see him, the poor soul in his weakness said, "Good sir, do you know this verse that General Taylor gave to me? It brought me to my Savior, and I die in peace." To Dr. Marsh's surprise, he repeated the lines:

> In peace let me resign my breath,
>   And thy salvation see;
> My sins deserve eternal death,
>   But Jesus died for me.

Think of the good that four simple lines can do. Be encouraged, you who know the healing power of the wounds of Jesus. Spread this truth by all means. Never mind how simple the language. Tell it. Tell it everywhere and in every way, even if you cannot do it in any other way than by copying a verse out of a hymnbook. Tell others that by the stripes of Jesus we are healed. May God bless you, dear friends!

2

The Beginning of Months

*And the LORD spake unto Moses and Aaron in
the land of Egypt, saying, This month shall be
unto you the beginning of months: it shall be the
first month of the year to you.*
—Exodus 12:1–2

When sinners put their trust in Jesus'
blood, they begin a whole new life.
Truly, they can count their day of
salvation as the first day of a new year and, in
fact, a new life. This is what happened with
Israel: the day of their exodus from Egypt
marked a new beginning, a new year, for them.
In fact, they changed their calendar; the month
they left Egypt became the first month of the
new year. I will attempt to further explain how
this happened.

In all probability, up to the time of the
Exodus, the new year began in autumn. People
have sometimes wondered at what season of

the year God created man. Many have decided that it must have been in autumn, so that when Adam was placed in the garden, he might at once find fruits ripe and ready to eat. It does not seem probable that he began his life while all the fruits were still raw and green. Therefore, many have concluded that the first year of human history began in the time of harvest, when fruits were mellowed for man's food.

For this reason, perhaps, in the old times the new year began when the feast of harvest was celebrated. However, here at the point of the Exodus, by a decree of God, the first day of the new year was changed. As far as Israel was concerned, the opening of the year would be in the time of our spring—in the month called Abib, or Nisan.

We know that a little before the barley was in the ear, and on the Sabbath after the Passover, the produce of the earth was so far advanced that the firstfruits were offered, and a sheaf of new barley was waved before the Lord. Of course, when I speak of spring and ears of barley, you must remember the difference of climate, for in that warm region the seasons are far in advance of ours. You must pardon me if my ideas become a little mixed; you can sort them easily at your leisure.

From the time when the Lord saved His people from destruction by passing them over, the ecclesiastical year began in the month Abib, in which the Passover was celebrated. The jubilee year was not altered but began in the autumnal equinox. The Jews seem to have had two or three beginnings of the year in relation to different purposes; but the ecclesiastical year, the great year by which Israel reckoned its existence, commenced henceforth in the month Abib, when the Lord brought His people "out of Egypt with a mighty hand, and with an outstretched arm" (Deut. 26:8).

God can change times and seasons as He pleases, and He has done so for great, commemorative purposes. The change of the Sabbath is along the same lines; for whereas the day of rest was formerly the seventh, it is now merged with the Lord's Day, which is the first day of the week. As Herbert said, "He did unhinge the day," and He set the Sabbath on golden hinges by consecrating the day of Christ's resurrection.

To every man God makes a similar change of times and seasons when He deals with him in a way of grace, for all things are become new within him (2 Cor. 5:17). Therefore, he begins a new chronology. We used to think our birthdays fell at certain times of the year; but now we regard with much more delight another day as our true birthday, since on that second birthday we began to truly live. Our calendar has been altered and amended by a deed of divine grace.

I want to bring to your mind this fact. Just as the people of Israel, when God gave them the Passover, had a complete shifting of all their dates, so when God gives a person the spiritual passover, a very wonderful change takes place in his chronology. Saved individuals date from the dawn of their true life—not from their first birthday, but from the day that they were born again. The Passover is, as we all know, a type of the great work of our redemption by the blood of Jesus, and it represents the personal application of Christ's blood to each believer. When we perceive the Lord's act of passing us over because of Christ's atoning sacrifice, then we begin to live, and from that day we date all future events.

This being said, I will, first, describe the Passover (see Exodus 12:1–32); second, mention varieties of its recurrence; and third, consider how the date of this grand event is to be regarded according to the law of the Lord.

THE MEANING OF THE PASSOVER

First, then, I will describe this remarkable event that was henceforth to stand at the head of the Jewish year and, indeed, at the commencement of Israel's chronology.

Salvation by Blood

First, the Passover was an act of salvation
by blood. You know how the elders and heads
of families each took a lamb and shut it up,
that they might examine it carefully. Having
chosen a lamb without blemish, in the prime of
its life (Exod. 12:5), they kept it by itself as a
separated and consecrated creature. After four
days they slew it and caught its blood in a basin. When this was done, they took hyssop and
dipped it in the blood and therewith sprinkled
the lintel and the two side posts of their houses
(Exod. 12:7). By this means the houses of Israel were preserved on that dark and dreadful
night, when with unsheathed sword the angel
of vengeance sped through every street of
Pharaoh's domain and slew the firstborn of all
the land, both of men and of cattle (Exod.
12:12).

You will remember, dear friends, the time
when you yourselves perceived that God's
vengeance was out against sin; you can even
now recollect your terror and your trembling.
Many of us can never forget the memorable
time when we first discovered that there was a
way of deliverance from the wrath of God.
Memory may drop all else from her enfeebled
grasp, but this is graven on the palms of her
hands.

Moses described our mode of deliverance when he described the Passover. The angel cannot be restrained, his wing cannot be bound, and his sword cannot be sheathed. He must go forth, and he must smite. He must smite us among the rest, for sin is upon us, and there must be no partiality: "The soul that sinneth, it shall die" (Ezek. 18:4).

But, do you remember when you discovered God's new way? Without abolishing the law, He has brought in a glorious, saving clause by which we can be ˙delivered. The clause is this, that if another would suffer instead of us and there was evidence that he had suffered, that would be enough for our deliverance.

Do you remember your joy at that discovery? If so, you can appreciate the feelings of the Israelites when they understood that God would accept an unblemished lamb in the place of their firstborn. If the blood was displayed upon the doorpost as the clear evidence that a sacrifice had suffered and died, then the angel would know that in that house his work was done and he could therefore pass over that habitation. The avenger was to demand a life, but the life was already paid, for there was the blood to prove it, and the avenger could go on his way. It was the night of God's Passover, not because the execution of vengeance was left undone in the houses passed over, but just the opposite. For in those houses the death-blow had been struck, and the victim had died, and, since the penalty could not be exacted twice, that family was clear.

I do not know whether there is any truth in the statement that lightning never strikes the same place twice. But, whether it is true or not, it is certain that wherever the lightning of God's vengeance has struck, it will not strike again. In each case where God's vengeance has struck the sinner's Substitute, it will not strike the sinner.

The best preservative for the Israelite's house was this: vengeance had struck there and could not strike again. There was the insurance mark, the streak of blood. Death had been there. Even though it had fallen on a harmless lamb, it had still fallen on a victim of God's own appointment. In God's eyes it had fallen upon Christ Himself, the "Lamb slain from [before] the foundation of the world" (Rev. 13:8). Because the claims of retribution had been fully met, there was no further demand, and Israel was secure. This is my eternal confidence, and here is my soul's sweet hymn:

> If thou hast my discharge procured,
> And freely in my room endured

The whole of wrath divine:
Payment God cannot twice demand,
First at my bleeding Surety's hand,
And then again at mine.

Turn then, my soul, unto thy rest;
The merits of thy great High Priest
Have bought thy liberty:
Trust in his efficacious blood,
Nor fear thy banishment from God,
Since Jesus died for thee.

For me, it was the beginning of my life, that day in which I discovered that judgment was passed upon me in the person of my Lord, and that "there is therefore now no condemnation to [me]" (Rom. 8:1). The law demands death: "The soul that sinneth, it shall die" (Ezek. 18:4). Christ gave what the law demands, and more. Christ, my Lord, has died, died in my place. It is written, "Who his own self bare our sins in his own body on the tree" (1 Pet. 2:24). Such a sacrifice is more than even the most rigorous law could demand. "Christ our passover is sacrificed for us" (1 Cor. 5:7). "Christ hath redeemed us from the curse of the law, being made a curse for us" (Gal. 3:13).

Therefore, we sit securely within doors, needing no guard without to drive away the destroyer; for when God sees the blood of Jesus, He will pass over us.

The Beginning of Months

*In his days Judah shall be saved, and
Israel shall dwell safely: and this is his
name whereby he shall be called, THE
LORD OUR RIGHTEOUSNESS.* (Jer. 23:6)

I say again, it was the beginning of life to
me when I saw Jesus as dying in my place. I
beheld the first sight that was worth beholding; let all the rest be darkness and like the
shadow of death. Then did my soul rejoice
when I understood and accepted the substitutionary sacrifice of the appointed Redeemer.
That is my first observation of the Passover:
the blood of sprinkling (Heb. 12:24) made Israel secure.

Refreshment from the Lamb

Here is my second observation: the night
of the Passover, the Israelites received refreshment from the lamb. Being saved by its
blood, the believing households stood and fed
upon the lamb. They never ate as they ate that
night. Those who spiritually understood the
symbol must have partaken of every morsel
with a mysterious awe mingled with an unfathomable delight. I am sure there must have
been a singular seriousness around the table as
they stood there eating in haste. Every now
and then they were startled by the shrieks that

rose from the Egyptian houses because of the slain of the Lord. It was a solemn feast, a meal of mingled hope and mystery.

Do you remember, brothers and sisters, when you first fed upon Christ, when your hungry spirit enjoyed the first morsel of that food of the soul? It was delicious food, was it not? It was better than angel's bread, for

> Never did angels taste above
> Redeeming grace and dying love.

I hope you have never risen from that table, but are daily feeding upon Jesus. It is a very instructive fact that we do not go to our Lord's table like the Israelites, to eat in haste with a staff in our hand (Exod. 12:11). But, we come there to recline at ease with our heads on His bosom, reposing in His love. Christ Jesus is the daily bread of our spirits.

Observe that the refreshment Israel ate that night was the Lamb "roast with fire" (Exod. 12:8). The best refreshment to a troubled heart is the suffering Savior, the Lamb roasted with fire. A poor sinner under conviction of sin goes to a place of worship, and he hears Christ preached as an example. This may be useful to the saint, but it is little help to the poor sinner. He cries, "That is true, but it rather condemns than comforts me." It is not food for him; he wants the Lamb roasted with fire, Christ his substitute, Christ suffering in his place and stead.

We hear a great deal about the beauty of Christ's moral character, and assuredly our blessed Lord deserves to be highly exalted for His character, but that is not the aspect under which He is food to a soul conscious of sin. The chief relish about our Lord Jesus to a penitent sinner is His sin-bearing and His agonies. We need the suffering Savior, the Christ of Gethsemane, the Christ of Golgotha and Calvary, Christ shedding His blood in the sinner's stead and bearing for us the fire of God's wrath. Nothing short of this will suffice to be food for a hungry heart. Withhold this, and you starve the child of God.

We are told in Exodus 12:9 that they were not to eat any of the lamb raw. Alas! There are some who try to do this with Christ, for they preach a half-atoning sacrifice. They try to make His person and His character to be food for their souls, but they have small liking for His passion. They cast His atonement into the background or represent it as an ineffective atonement that does not rescue any soul. What is this but to devour a raw Christ?

I will not touch their half-roasted lamb; I will have nothing to do with their half substitution, their half-complete redemption. No, no.

Give me a Savior who has borne all my sins in
His own body (1 Pet. 2:24) and so has been
roasted with fire to the full. "It is finished"
(John 19:30) is the most charming note in all
of Calvary's music. "It is finished." The fire
has passed upon the Lamb. He has borne the
whole of the wrath that was due to His people.
This is the royal dish of the feast of love.

There are a multitude of teachers who
want to have the Lamb boiled with water,
though the Scripture says, "Eat not of it raw,
nor sodden at all with water" (Exod. 12:9). I
have heard it said that a great number of ser-
mons are about Christ and the Gospel yet neither Christ nor His Gospel are preached in
them. If so, the preachers present the Lamb
boiled in the water of their own thoughts and
speculations and notions.

Now, the harm in this boiling process is
that the water takes away a good deal from the
meat. Likewise, philosophical discourses on the
Lord Jesus take away much of the essence and
virtue of His person, offices, work, and glory.
The real juice and vital nutrients of His glorious Word are carried off by interpretations
that do not explain, but explain away. How
many boil away the soul of the Gospel by their
carnal wisdom!

What is worse still, when meat is boiled,
not only does the meat get into the water, but

the water gets into the meat. So, what truth
these gospel-boilers do hand out is boiled with
error, and you receive from them dishes made
up partly of God's truth and partly of men's
imaginings. We hear in some measure solid
Gospel and in larger measure mere watery reasoning. When certain preachers preach atonement, it is not pure and simple substitution;
one hardly knows what it is. Their atonement
is not the vicarious sacrifice, but a perform-
ance of a long list of things. They have a theory
that is like the remainders of meat after days
of boiling, all strings and fibers.

People use all kinds of schemes to try to
extract the marrow and fatness from the
grand, soul-satisfying doctrine of substitution,
which to my mind is the choicest truth that
can ever be brought forth for the food of souls.
I cannot figure out why so many preachers are
afraid of the shedding of blood for the remis-
sion of sin (Matt. 26:28). Why do they have to
stew down the most important of all the truths
of revelation?

As the type could only be correct when the
lamb was roasted with fire, so the Gospel is not
truly presented unless we describe our Lord
Jesus in His sufferings in the place of sinners.
He was absolutely and literally a substitution
for them. When it comes to the Gospel, I will
allow no dilution: it is substitution. He bore

our sins (1 Pet. 2:24). He was made sin for us (2 Cor. 5:21). "The chastisement of our peace was upon him; and with his stripes we are healed" (Isa. 53:5). We must have no mystifying of this plain truth. It must not be "sodden at all with water" (Exod. 12:9). We must have Christ in His sufferings, fresh from the fire.

Now, this is the lamb they were to eat, and they were to eat all of it. Not a morsel was to be left (Exod. 12:10). Oh, that you and I would never cut and divide Christ so as to choose one part of Him and leave another! Let not a bone of Him be broken (Exod. 12:46), but let us take the whole Christ, up to the full measure of our capacity. Prophet, Priest, and King, Christ divine and Christ human, Christ loving and living, Christ dying, Christ risen, Christ ascended, Christ coming again, Christ triumphant over all His foes—the whole Lord Jesus Christ is ours. We must not reject a single morsel of what is revealed concerning Him, but we must feed on it all as we are able.

That night Israel had to feed on the lamb there and then. They could not save a portion for the next day; they had to consume it all one way or another (Exod. 12:10). Oh, my friend, we need a whole Christ at this very moment. Let us receive Him in His entirety. Oh, for a splendid appetite and good digestion to receive into my inmost soul the Lord's Christ just as I find Him.

May you and I never think lightly of our Lord in any of His offices or aspects. All that you now know and all that you can find out concerning Christ, you should now believe, appreciate, feed on, and rejoice in. Make the most of all that is in the Word concerning your Lord. Let Him enter into your being to become part and parcel of yourself. If you do this, the day in which you feed on Jesus will be the first day of your life, its day of days, the day from which you date all that follows. If once you have fed upon Christ Jesus, you will never forget it in time or in eternity.

Refreshment from the lamb was the second event that was celebrated in each succeeding Passover.

Purification from Leaven

The third event was the purification of their houses from leaven. (See Exodus 12:15.) This was to go side by side with the sprinkling of the blood and the eating of the lamb. They were told that they must not eat leaven for seven days, for whoever ate leaven would be "cut off from Israel" (Exod. 12:15). This purification was deeply important, for it is put in equal position with the sprinkling of the blood.

The two could not be separated. Anyone who divided the two faced the pain and penalty of being divided from the congregation of Israel.

Now, it is always a pity to preach justification by faith in a way that makes sanctification a part of justification. But, it is also a horrible error to preach justification in a way that denies the absolute necessity of sanctification. The two are joined together by the Lord. There must be the eating of the lamb and the sprinkling of the blood, and there must be the purging out of the old leaven as well. Carefully, the Jews looked into every closet, corner, drawer, and cupboard to sweep out every crumb of stale bread. If they had any bread, even if it was new and they intended to eat it, they had to put it all away, for there could not be a particle of leaven in the same house with the lamb.

When you and I first came to Christ, what a sweeping out there was of the leaven! I know I was fully delivered from the leaven of the Pharisees (Luke 12:1), for all trust in my own good works went, even the last crumb of it. All confidence in rites and ceremonies went, too. I do not have a crust left of these sour and corrupt confidences at the present moment, and I wish never to taste that old leaven again. Some people are always chewing on that leaven, glorying in their own prayers and giving and ceremonies; but when Christ comes in, this leaven all goes out. The leaven of the Pharisees, which is hypocrisy (Luke 12:1), must be cleared out.

> *Blessed is he whose transgression is for-*
> *given, whose sin is covered. Blessed is*
> *the man unto whom the LORD imputeth*
> *not iniquity, and in whose spirit there is*
> *no guile.*   *(Ps. 32:1–2)*

Guile must go, or guilt will not go. The Lord sweeps the cunning, the craftiness, and the deceit out of His people. He makes them true before His face. They wish that they were as clear of every sin as they are from insincerity. They once tried to dwell before the Lord with double-dealing, pretending to be what they were not. But as soon as they ate of Christ and the blood was sprinkled, then they humbled themselves in truth and laid bare their sinfulness and stood before God as they were, with their hypocrisy torn away.

Christ has not saved the man who still trusts in falsehood. You cannot feed on Christ and at the same time hold love of sin or vain confidence in yourself. Self and sin must go. But, oh, what a day it is when the old leaven is thrown out. We will never forget it! That month is the beginning of months, the first month of the year to us, when the Spirit of truth purges out the spirit of falsehood.

A Mighty Deliverance

We come now to our fourth point about the Passover. On the passover night there came, as the result of these other things, a wonderful, glorious, and mighty deliverance. That night every Israelite was promised immediate emancipation, and as soon as the morning dawned, he left his house and Egypt, too. He left the brick kilns forever, he washed the brick earth from his hands for the last time, and he left the yoke he used to carry when he worked amid the clay. He looked at the Egyptian taskmaster, remembered how he had often struck him with the stick, and rejoiced that he would never strike him again, for the taskmaster was at his feet begging him to leave lest all Egypt should die. Oh, what joy!

They marched out with their unleavened bread on their backs (Exod. 12:34), for they still had some days in which they were to eat it, and I think before the seventh day of unleavened bread was over (Exod. 13:6–7) they had reached the Red Sea. Still eating unleavened bread, they went down into the depths of the Red Sea. Still with no flavor of leaven in their mouths, they stood on its shore to sing to the Lord the great hallelujah. God had "triumphed gloriously: the horse and his rider [had] he thrown into the sea" (Exod. 15:1).

Do you recollect when the Lord purged you from love of sin and trust in self, when He brought you completely out and set you free, and when He said, "Go on to the promised rest; go on to Canaan"? Do you remember when you saw your sins drowned forever, never to rise in judgment against you? Not merely was your destruction prevented, not merely was your soul fed with the finest food, not merely was your heart and your house cleansed of hypocrisy, but you, yourself, were delivered and emancipated, the Lord's free man! Oh, if you remember, I am sure you will acknowledge the wisdom of the Lord's decree: "This month shall be unto you the beginning of months: it shall be the first month of the year to you" (Exod. 12:2).

This much will suffice in describing the event of the Passover.

HOW WE CELEBRATE THE PASSOVER TODAY

Now, secondly, I want to mention the ways in which the Passover reoccurs among us today. There are three ways: the salvation of ourselves, our families, and our world.

Power in the Blood

Our Personal Salvation

The first recurrence is, of course, the personal salvation of each one of us. All of Exodus 12 was transacted in your heart and mine when we first knew the Lord.

A venerable elder in my church, Mr. White, said to me the other night, "Oh, sir, it is very precious to read the Bible, but it is infinitely more delightful to have it here in your own heart." Now, I find it very profitable to read about the Passover; but, oh, how sweet to have a passover transacted in your own soul by the work of the Holy Spirit!

Moses wrote thousands of years ago about something that happened, but the substance of it has happened to me in all its details, and to thousands who are trusting in the Lord. Can we not read this story in Exodus and say, "Yes, it is so even now"? Every word of it is true, for it has all occurred to me, every atom of it, even to the eating of the bitter herbs (Exod. 12:8). For I recall that, at the very moment that I tasted the sweet flavor of my Lord's atonement, I also felt the bitterness of repentance from sin and the bitterness of struggling against the temptation to sin again. Even the minute touches of that festival are symbolic of salvation, as thousands of Christians can testify. This passover record is not a story of

58

olden times alone; it is the record of your life and mine. I hope it is. Thus, by each separate saved man the Passover Feast is kept.

The Salvation of Our Families

In a certain sense, the Passover occurs again when a man's family is saved. Remember, the Passover was a family business. The father and mother were present when the lamb was slain. I dare say the oldest son helped to bring the lamb to the slaughter; another held the knife; a third held the basin; the little boy fetched the bunch of hyssop; and they all united in the sacrifice. They all saw the father strike the lintel and the doorposts, and they all ate of the lamb that night. Everyone that was in the house, all that were part of the family, partook of the meal. They were all protected by the blood, they were all refreshed by the feast, and they all started out the next morning to go to Canaan.

Have you ever held a family supper of that kind? "Oh," some fathers might say, "it would be the beginning of family life to me if all my sons and daughters sitting around my supper table were saved. Oh, that all my children truly belonged to Christ." A family begins to live in the highest sense when as a family, without exception, it has all been redeemed, all sprinkled with the blood, all made to feed on Jesus, all purged from sin, and all freed to leave the domains of sin, bound for the kingdom. What joy! "I have no greater joy than to hear that my children walk in truth" (3 John 1:4). If any of you enjoy the privilege of family salvation, you may well set up a monument of praise and make a generous offering to God, who favors you in this way. Engrave it on marble and set it up forever! This household is saved, and the day of its salvation is the beginning of its spiritual history.

The Salvation of Our World

Extend the thought: the Passover was not only a family ordinance, but it was for all the tribes of Israel. There were many families, but in every house the passover lamb was sacrificed. It would be an impressive thing if you business owners could gather all your workers together and say, "All of these workers understand the sprinkling of the blood, and all of them feed on Christ." Dear men and women who are placed in such responsible positions, you could indeed say, "This will be the beginning of months to us." Labor for it, therefore, and make it your heart's desire.

The Beginning of Months

If you live to see the district in which you labor permeated with the Gospel, what a joy! Oh, that we might live to see every house in our communities sprinkled with the redeeming blood! Oh, that we might live to see the whole country feasting. I do not mean the feasting done at Christmas, when many eat sweets to excess; I mean feasting spiritually upon Christ, where there can be no excess. Oh, what a beginning of years it would be for our country! What a paradise it would be! If it were so in any country, what a day to be remembered! Commence a nation's annals from its evangelization. Begin the chronicle of a people from the day when they bow at the feet of Jesus.

There will come a day to this poor earth when Jesus will reign over all of it (Rev. 11:15). It may be a long time yet, but the day will come when Christ will have "dominion... from sea to sea" (Ps. 72:8). The nations that are called Christian, although they so little deserve the title, already date their chronology from the birth of Christ. This is a sort of faint foreshadowing of the way in which people will one day date all things from the reign of Jesus. His kingdom will come yet. God has decreed His triumph, and on the wings of time it hastens. When He comes, that month will be the beginning of months to us.

HOW TO REGARD OUR PASSOVER

Now, for my last point, I will show how we should regard our Passover, the day of our salvation.

The Most Honorable Day

Primarily, the day in which we first knew the Savior as the Passover Lamb should always be the most honorable day that has ever dawned upon us. The Israelites placed the month Abib as the first month because it was the month of the Passover. Mark the date you came to know the Lord as the premier day, the noblest hour you have ever known. It eclipses your natural birthday, for then you were born in sin, then you were "born unto trouble, as the sparks fly upward" (Job 5:7). But now you are born into spiritual life, born unto eternal bliss.

Your salvation day eclipses your marriage day, for union to Christ will bring you greater joy than the happiest of marriage bonds. If you have ever received the honors of the State, gained distinction in learning, attained a position in society, or arrived at a larger wealth, all these are but dim, cloudy, foggy days compared with this "morning without clouds" (2 Sam. 23:4). On that day, your sun rose, never to go down again. The die was cast. Your destiny for glory was openly declared.

I entreat you to never degrade that blessed day in your thoughts by thinking more of any pleasure, honor, or advancement than you do of the blessing of salvation by the blood of Jesus. I am afraid that some of you are striving and struggling after other distinctions, and you think that if you could only reach a certain event you would be satisfied. Is your salvation not worth vastly more than this? You feel that you would be set for life if a certain matter turned out right. Friend, you were set for life when you were made anew in Christ Jesus. You came to your estate when you came to Christ. You were promoted when He received you into His friendship. You gained all that you need desire when you found Christ. A saint of old said, "He is all my salvation, and all my desire."

If you should be elected to some high position in the government, do not think that the event would overshadow your conversion. Think of your salvation as the Lord thinks of it, for He says, "Since thou wast precious in my sight, thou hast been honourable, and I have loved thee" (Isa. 43:4). Honor belongs to those who believe in Jesus. In Jesus you boast and glory, and so you should. The mark of blood is a believer's chief adornment and decoration, and his being cleansed and set free by grace is his noblest distinction. Glory in grace and in nothing else. Prize the work of grace beyond all the treasures of Egypt.

The Beginning of Life

The date of your salvation is to be regarded as the beginning of life. The Israelites reckoned that all their former existence as a nation had been death. The brick kilns of Egypt, the sitting around pots of meat, the mixing with idolaters, the hearing of a language they did not understand—all Egyptian life they considered to be death, and the month that ended it was to them the beginning of months. On the other hand, they looked on all that followed their exodus as life. The Passover was the beginning, and only the beginning. A beginning implies that something is to follow.

Now then, Christians, whenever you speak about your existence before conversion, always do it with shamefacedness, as one risen from the dead might speak of the cemetery and the worm of corruption. I feel grieved when people stand up and talk about what they used to do before they were converted as an old sailor talks of his voyages and storms. No, no! Be ashamed of your "former lusts in your ignorance" (1 Pet. 1:14). If you must speak of them to the praise and glory of Christ, speak with tears and sighs and bated breath. Death, rottenness, and corruption are all most fitly left in silence; or if they demand a voice, let it be as solemn and mournful as a funeral service. Tell about your sinful past in a way that will show that you wish it had never happened. Let your conversion be the burial of the old existence (2 Cor. 5:17). As for that which follows after, take care that you make it real life, worthy of the grace that has saved you.

Suppose these Israelites had loitered in Egypt. Suppose one of them had said, "Well, I did not finish that batch of bricks. I cannot leave just yet. I would like to see them thoroughly baked and prepared for the pyramid." What a foolish man he would have been! No, they left the bricks and the clay and the stuff behind; they left right away and let Egypt take care of itself.

Now, child of God, leave the ways of sin with determination. Leave the world; leave its pleasures; leave its cares; and get right away to Jesus and His leadership. You are now the Lord's free man. Will the Lamb be slain and mean nothing? Will the blood be sprinkled for nothing? Will the leavened bread be purged out in vain? Will the Red Sea be crossed, and the

Egyptians drowned, and you remain a slave? The thought is abhorrent.

That was the wrongdoing of the Israelites: they still had a craving for the leeks and garlic of Egypt (Num. 11:5). These strong-smelling things had scented their garments, and it is hard to get such vile odors out of one's clothes. Alas, the Egyptian garlic clings to us, and its smell is not always so abominable to us as it ought to be.

Besides, they pined for fish that they ate in plenty in Egypt (Num. 11:5), muddy fish though it was. There were better fisheries for them in Jordan and Gennesaret and the Great Sea if they had gone ahead. Sweeter herbs were on Canaan's hills than ever grew in Egypt's mire. Because of this evil lusting, they were kept dodging about for forty years in the wilderness (Num. 32:13). They might have marched into Canaan in forty days had it not been for that stinking garlic of theirs. Their Egyptian habits and memories held them back. Oh, that God would cut us completely free and enable us to forget those things of which we are now ashamed (Rom. 6:21)!

Setting All Things Right

Inasmuch as the Passover became the beginning of the year to Israel, it set all things right. I told you that the year had formerly begun in autumn, according to most traditions. Was this really the best season to start the year? Was autumn the best season in which to begin life, with winter all ahead and everything declining?

With the institution of the Passover, the year was made to begin in what is our spring. When could the year begin more fitly than in the springtide of early May? It seems to me that the year actually does begin in spring. I do not see that the year naturally begins in winter, though it does so arbitrarily. In the middle of winter, the year as yet lies dead. When the birds sing and the flowers rise from their beds of earth, then the year begins.

I think it is a wrong supposition that our first parents commenced life in autumn, amid lengthening nights and declining forces. No, by all means let the date be fixed in spring. Then the salutations of the new year will be sweet with fragrant flowers and rich with joyous songs. Moreover, the time of spring in the East is not a season without crops, for in April and May the first ears of corn are ready, and many other fruits are fit for food.

It was good for the Israelites to have the Feast of Firstfruits in the month Abib. Hence, they could bring the first ears to the Lord and not wait until they were ripe before they blessed the Giver of all good. We ought to be grateful for green mercies and not wait until everything comes to ripeness.

In some parts of the East there is fruit all year round, and why not in Eden? In my delightful country England, which bears a very close resemblance to the East, one tree or another bears fruit every month all year round. So, if Adam had been created in the month of April, there would have been food for him, followed by a succession of fruits that would have supplied all his wants. Then he would have had summer before him with all its ripening beauties. This is a more paradisiacal outlook than winter.

It is right that the year should begin with the firstfruits, and I am sure it is quite right that the year should begin for you and me when we come to Christ and receive the firstfruits of the Spirit (Rom. 8:23). Everything is in disarray until a man knows Christ. Everything is disorderly and bottom upwards until the Gospel comes and turns everything upside down, and then the right side is up again. Man is all wrong until the Gospel puts him all right.

Though grace is above nature, it is not contrary to nature; rather, it restores true nature. Our nature is never so truly the nature of a man as when it is no longer man's sinful nature. We truly become men, such as God meant men to be, when we cease to be the kind of men that sin has made men to be.

Since our life begins at our spiritual passover and at our feeding upon Christ, we ought to always regard our conversion as a festival and remember it with praise. Whenever we look back on it, the memory of it should excite delight in our hearts.

How long should a person thank God for forgiving his sins? Is life long enough? Is time long enough? Is eternity long enough? How long should a man thank God for saving him from going down to hell? Would fifty years suffice? Oh, no, that would never do; the blessing is too great to all be sung of in a millennium.

Suppose you and I never had a single mercy except this one, that we were made the children of God and coheirs with Christ Jesus (Rom. 8:16–17). Suppose we had nothing else to enjoy. We ought to sing about that alone forever and ever. Yes, if we were sick, cast on the bed of pain with a hundred diseases, with the bone wearing through the skin, yet since God's everlasting mercy would sanctify every pain, should we not still continue to lift up happy psalms to God and praise Him forever and ever? Therefore, let this be your slogan all through the year: "Hallelujah! Praise the Lord!"

Power in the Blood

The Israelites always closed the Passover with a hymn of praise; therefore, let us close this chapter with holy joy and continue our happy music until this year ends, yes, until time shall be no more. Amen.

3

God's Watchful Care

*The eyes of the LORD thy God are always
upon it, from the beginning of the year
even unto the end of the year.
—Deuteronomy 11:12*

*T*ruly, salvation does start a new year for
the new believer. And the eyes of the
Lord are upon His new child from the
beginning of that new year to the end, and
throughout every year that follows. Our text,
Deuteronomy 11:12, assures us of this. But, to
fully understand our text, let us look at the
land to which it refers, Palestine.

Palestine was a land that was superior to
Egypt. Egypt was a land that produced food for
its inhabitants only by the laborious process of
irrigating its fields. The Israelites, during their
sojourn in Egypt, mingled with the Egyptians
as they watched with anxious eyes the swelling
of the river Nile. They shared in the incessant

labors of preserving water in reservoirs and then slowly eking it out to nourish the various crops.

Moses told the Israelites in Deuteronomy 11 that the land of Palestine was not at all like Egypt. It was a land that did not depend so much on the labor of the inhabitants as on the good will of God. Moses called it a land of hills and valleys, a land of springs and rivers, a land dependent not on the rivers of earth, but on the rain of heaven (Deut. 11:10–11). He described it in conclusion as

> *A land which the LORD thy God careth for: the eyes of the LORD thy God are always upon it, from the beginning of the year even unto the end of the year.*
>
> *(Deut. 11:12)*

Egypt is a type of the natural man, and Canaan is a type of the spiritual man. In this world the merely carnal man has to be his own providence and look to himself for all his needs. Hence, his cares are always many, and frequently they become so heavy that they drive him to desperation. He lives a life of care, anxiety, sorrow, fretfulness, and disappointment. He dwells in Egypt, and he knows that there is no joy or comfort or provision if he does not wear out his soul in winning it.

But, the spiritual man dwells in another country; his faith makes him a citizen of Canaan. It is true he endures the same toils and experiences and afflictions as the ungodly, but they affect him differently, for they come as a gracious Father's appointments, and they go at the bidding of loving wisdom. By faith the godly man casts his care upon God, who cares for him (1 Pet. 5:7). He walks without heavy cares because he knows he is the child of heaven's loving-kindness, for whom "all things work together for good" (Rom. 8:28). God is his great Guardian and Friend, and all his concerns are safe in the hands of infinite grace.

Even in the year of drought, the believer dwells in green pastures and lies down beside still waters (Ps. 23:2). As for the ungodly, he abides in the wilderness and hears the mutterings of that curse:

> *Cursed be the man that trusteth in man, and maketh flesh his arm...he shall be like the heath in the desert, and shall not see when good cometh. (Jer. 17:5–6)*

Do you disagree that Canaan is a fitting type of the present condition of the Christian? I have frequently insisted that it is a far better type of the Christian soldier on earth than of the glorified saint in heaven. Canaan is sometimes used in our hymns as the picture of heaven, but it is not so. A moment's reflection will show that Canaan is distinctly the picture of the present state of every believer.

While we are under conviction of sin, we are like Israel in the wilderness; we have no rest for our feet. But, when we put our trust in Jesus, we do, as it were, cross the river and leave the wilderness behind. "We which have believed do enter into rest" (Heb. 4:3), for "there remaineth therefore a rest to the people of God" (Heb. 4:9).

Believers have entered into the finished salvation that is provided for us in Christ Jesus. The blessings of our inheritance are to a great extent already in our possession. The state of salvation is no longer a land of promise, but it is a land possessed and enjoyed. We have peace with God; we are even now justified by faith (Rom. 5:1). "Beloved, now are we the sons of God" (1 John 3:2). We are sons right now! Covenant blessings are at this moment actually ours, just as the land of Canaan was actually possessed by Israel.

It is true there is an enemy in Canaan, an enemy to be driven out. There is indwelling sin, which is entrenched in our hearts like troops in walled cities. There are fleshly lusts, which are like chariots of iron with which we have to war. Even so, the land is ours. We have the covenanted heritage at this moment in our possession. The foes who would rob us of it will be utterly rooted out by the sword of faith and the weapon of all prayer.

The Christian, like Israel in Canaan, is not under the government of Moses now; he is done with Moses once and for all. Moses was magnified and made honorable as he made his last climb to the top of the hill, and with a kiss from God's lips he was carried into heaven. (See Deuteronomy 34:1, 5.) Even so, the law has been magnified and made honorable in the person of Christ, and it has ceased to reign over the believer.

As Joshua was the leader of the Israelites when they came into Canaan, so Jesus is our leader now. It is He who leads us on from victory to victory. He will not sheathe His sword until He has given us all the holiness and happiness that the covenant promises us. For these and many other reasons, it is clear that the children of Israel in Canaan were a type of us believers.

Beloved, those of you who are believers will relish the text. It is to believers that the text is addressed. "The eyes of the LORD thy God are always upon [you, believer] from the beginning of the year even unto the end of the year" (Deut. 11:12). You who trust in Jesus are under the guidance of the great Joshua. You are fighting sin. You have obtained salvation. You have left the wilderness of conviction and fear behind you, and you have come into the Canaan of faith. Now the eyes of God are upon you and upon your state from the opening of the year to its close.

May the Holy Spirit bless us as we study the text in more detail. We will, first, take the text as we find it. Second, we will turn the text around. Third, we will blot the text out. Then, fourth, we will distill practical lessons from the text.

GOD'S WATCHFUL EYES

First, we will consider the text as we find it. The first word that glitters before us like a jewel in a crown is that word *eyes*—"the eyes of the LORD" (Deut. 11:12). What is meant here? Surely not mere omniscience. In that sense "the eyes of the LORD are in every place, beholding the evil and the good" (Prov. 15:3). God sees Hagar as well as Sarah; He beholds Judas when he gives the traitorous kiss (Matt. 26:48–49) just as surely as He beholds the holy woman when she washes the Savior's feet with her tears (Luke 7:37–38).

No, our text is speaking of something more than omniscience; there is love in the text to sweeten observation. "The LORD knoweth the way of the righteous" (Ps. 1:6) with a knowledge that is over and above that of omniscience. The eyes of the Lord are upon the righteous, not merely to see them, but to view them with delight; not only to observe them, but to observe them with affectionate care and interest.

An Intense Affection

The meaning of the text is then, first, that God's love is always upon His people. Oh, Christians, think of this (it is rather to be thought of than to be spoken of), that God loves us! The big heart of Deity is set upon us poor, insignificant, undeserving, worthless beings. God loves us, loves us ever, never thinks of us without loving thoughts. He never regards us, nor speaks of us, nor acts towards us, except in love.

God is love in a certain sense towards all, for He is full of benevolence to all His creatures. Love is indeed His essence. But, there is a depth unfathomable when the word *love* is used in reference to His elect ones. They are the objects of distinguishing grace, redeemed by blood, set free by power, adopted by condescension, and preserved by faithfulness. Beloved, do not ask me to write of this love, but implore God the Holy Spirit to speak of it to your inmost souls. The loving eyes of God are always upon you, the poorest and most obscure of His people, from the beginning of the year even to the end (Deut. 11:12).

A Personal Interest

The text teaches us that the Lord takes a personal interest in us. It does not say that God loves us and therefore sends an angel to protect and watch over us, but the Lord does it Himself. The eyes that observe us are God's own eyes; the guardian under whose protection we are placed is God Himself. Some mothers give their children to others to feed and care for, but God never does. All His babes are fed by Him and are carried in His own arms.

We could do little if we had to perform everything personally, and therefore most things are done by proxy. The captain, when the vessel is to be steered across the deep, must have his hour of sleep; and then the second in command, or someone else, must manage the vessel. But, in times of emergency the captain himself is called up and takes personal responsibility. See him as he himself anxiously heaves the lead and stands at the helm or at the lookout, for he can trust no one else in perilous moments.

It seems from the text that it is always a time of emergency with God's people, for their great Lord always exercises a personal care over them. He has never said to His angels, "I will dispense with my own watching, and you will guard my saints." While He gives angels charge concerning His people (Ps. 91:11), yet He Himself is personally their keeper and their shield. "I the LORD do keep it; I will water it every moment: lest any hurt it, I will keep it night and day" (Isa. 27:3).

Think of times when you have been very sick and have sent for a physician. Perhaps the doctor was busy with another patient and sent his assistant, who was probably just as skillful. Yet, as soon as that assistant came, such was your confidence in the doctor himself that you felt quite disappointed. You wanted to see the man who treated you successfully in days gone by.

We need not fear that God will send someone else. Oh, beloved, when I think of the text, I am of the same mind as Moses when God said, "I will send an angel before thee" (Exod. 33:2). "No," Moses said, "that will not suffice. 'If thy presence go not with me, carry us not up hence' (Exod. 33:15)." My Lord, I cannot be satisfied with Gabriel or Michael; I cannot be content with the brightest of the seraphim who stand before Your throne. It is Your presence I want, and blessed be Your name, it is Your presence that the text promises to give.

The anxious mother is glad to have a careful nurse on whom she can rely. But, in the crisis of her baby's disease, when his life trembles in the balance, she says, "Nurse, I must sit up with the child myself tonight." And though it is perhaps the third or fourth night since the mother has had sleep, yet her eyes will not close as long as the point of danger is still in view.

See, my friends, see the loving tenderness of our gracious God. Never, never, never, does He delegate the care of His people to others, no matter how good or powerful they are. His own eyes, without a substitute, must watch over us.

An Unwearied Power

Further, the text reminds us of the unwearied power of God towards His people. What? Can His eyes always watch us? This would not be possible if He were not God. To concentrate always on one object, man can scarcely accomplish that. But, where there are ten thousand times ten thousand objects, how can the same eyes always be upon every one of them?

I know what unbelief has said to you. It has whispered, "He brings forth the stars. 'He calleth them all by their names' (Ps. 147:4). How then can He notice a small insect like you?" Perhaps you have replied, "My way is unseen by God. God has forgotten me. My God has forsaken me." But, this is where the text comes in. Not only has He not forgotten you, but He has never once taken His eyes off you! Though you are one among so many, yet He has observed you as narrowly, as carefully, as tenderly as if you were the only child in the divine family. He has heard you as if you were the only one whose prayers were to be heard and whose cares were to be relieved.

What would you think about yourself if you were the only saved soul in the world, the only elect one of God, the only one purchased on the bloody cross? Why, you would say, "How God must care for me! How He must watch over me! Surely, He will never take His eyes off such a special favorite." Beloved, though God's family is so large, it is the same as if you were the only one. The eyes of the Lord never grow weary. He "shall neither slumber nor sleep" (Ps. 121:4). Both by day and by night He observes each one of His people.

Accepted in Christ

If you put these things together—intense affection, personal interest, and unwearied power—and if you remember that God's heart is moved towards you by unchanging purposes of grace, surely there will be enough to make you lose yourself in wonder, love, and praise. You have sinned in the past, but your sin has never made Him love you less. He never looked at you as you are in yourself, naked and standing alone, but He saw you and loved you in Christ, even when you were "dead in trespasses and sins" (Eph. 2:1). He has seen you in Christ ever since and has never ceased to love you.

It is true you have been very faulty (what tears this ought to cost you!), but as He never loved you for your good works, He has never cast you away for your bad works. He has beheld you as washed in the atoning blood of Jesus until you have become whiter than snow (Isa. 1:18), and He has seen you clothed in the perfect righteousness of your Substitute. (See Isaiah 61:10.) Therefore, He has looked upon you and regarded you as though you were without "spot, or wrinkle, or any such thing" (Eph. 5:27).

Grace has always set you before the Lord's eyes as being in His dear Son and therefore all fair and lovely—a pleasing prospect for Him to look upon. He has gazed upon you, beloved, but never with anger. He has looked upon you when your weakness, no, your willful wickedness, has made you hate yourself. Yet, though He has seen you in this sad state, He has had such a regard for your relationship to Christ that you have still been "accepted in the beloved" (Eph. 1:6).

I wish my mortal words could convey the full glory of that thought, but they cannot. You must eat this morsel alone. You must take it like a wafer made with honey and put it under your tongue and suck the sweetness out of it. The eyes of God, my God, are always upon His chosen. They are eyes of affection, delight, unwearied power, immutable wisdom, and unchanging love.

HIS CONSTANT CARE

The next word that seems to flash and sparkle in the text is that word *always*. "The eyes of the LORD thy God are always upon it" (Deut. 11:12). And it is added, as if that word were not enough for such dull ears as ours, "from the beginning of the year even unto the end of the year" (Deut. 11:12). This is so plain and pointed that we cannot imagine we are removed from God's eyes even for a single day or a single hour of the day or a single minute of the hour.

I tried to discover the other day what time of life we could afford to be without God.

Perhaps imagination suggests the time of prosperity, when business prospers, wealth is growing, and the mind is happy. Ah, beloved, to be without our God then, would be like the marriage feast without the bridegroom! It would be the day of delight and no delight, a sea and no water in it, a day and no light. What? All these mercies and no God? Then there is only a shell but no kernel, a shadow but no substance.

When a person has earthly "joys" but none of the Lord's presence, his soul can hear satanic laughter. Satan laughs at the soul because it has tried to make the world its rest and is sure to be deceived. Do without God in prosperity, beloved? We cannot, for then we would grow worldly, proud, and careless; and deep damnation would be our lot. The Christian in prosperity is like a man standing on a pinnacle. He must be divinely upheld, or his fall will be terrible. If you can do without God at all, it certainly is not when you are standing on the pinnacle.

What then? Could we do without Him in adversity? Ask the heart that is breaking! Ask the tortured spirit that has been deserted by its friend! Ask the child of poverty who has nowhere to lay his head! Ask the daughter of sickness, tossing by night and day on that uneasy bed! Ask them, "Could you do without your God?" And the very thought causes wailing and gnashing of teeth. *With* God pain becomes pleasure, and dying beds are elevated into thrones. But, *without* God—ah, what could we do?

Well, then, is there no period during which we could do without God? Cannot the young Christian, full of freshness and vigor, elated with the novelty of piety, do without his God? Ah, poor puny thing, how can the lamb do without the shepherd to carry it in his arms? Cannot the man in midlife then, whose virtues have been strengthened, do without his God? No, he tells you that it is his day of battle and that the darts fly thickly in business and that the burdens of life are heavy. Without God, a man in midlife is like a naked man in the midst of a thicket of briars and thorns; he cannot hope to get through without being torn and scratched and mangled.

Ask the elderly man with all the experience of seventy years whether he has attained to an independence of grace. He will say to you that as his body grows weaker, it is his joy that his inner man is renewed day by day (2 Cor. 4:16). But, take away God, who is the spring of that renewal, and old age would be utter wretchedness.

Ah, friend, there is not a moment in any one day that you or I have ever lived, that we could have afforded to dispense with the help of God. For when we have thought ourselves strong, as, alas, we have been fools enough to do, in five minutes we have done that which has cost us rivers of tears to undo. In an unguarded moment we have spoken a word that we could not recall, but that we would have recalled if we had to bite our tongues in halves to do so. We have thought a thought that has gone speeding through our souls like a hellish thunderbolt, making a fiery path along the spirit. The evil thought would have become a terrible act if God, whom we had forgotten, had forgotten us.

We need to "set the LORD always before [us]" (Ps. 16:8). Let us then, when we wake in the morning, take the promise in Deuteronomy 11:12 and say, "Lord, You have said You will always be with us. Then do not leave us until the dews of evening fall and we return to our beds. Do not leave us even then, lest temptation is whispered in our ears in the night and we wake to defile our minds with unholiness. Do not leave us ever, O God, but always be our very present help (Ps. 46:1)!"

Perhaps you have had the gloomiest year of your life. Perhaps the latest newspapers have been like the prophetic scroll that was written within and without with lamentations. (See Ezekiel 2:9–10.) Take comfort; a new year is on its way. Yet, there is no guarantee that next year will be an improvement. Who can tell?

Well, friends, let it be what God chooses it to be. Let it be what He appoints. For there is this comfort: not a moment from the first of January to the thirty-first of December will be without the tender care of heaven. Not even for a second will the Lord remove His eyes from any one of His people. Here is good cheer for us! We will march boldly into this wilderness, for the pillar of fire and cloud will never leave us. The manna will never cease to come. The rock that followed us will never cease to flow with living streams. Onward, onward, let us go, joyously confident in our God.

JEHOVAH'S EYES

The next word that springs from the text is that great word *Jehovah*. It is a pity that our translators did not give us the names of God as they found them in the original. The word LORD in capitals is good enough, but that grand and glorious name of *Jehovah* should have been retained. Then we would read in Deuteronomy 11:12, "The eyes of Jehovah are always upon it." He who surveys us with love and care is none other than the one indivisible God. We should conclude that if we have His eyes to view us, we have His heart to love us. If we have His heart to love us, we have His wings to cover us (Ps. 91:4), and we have His hands to bear us up, and we have the everlasting arms to be underneath us (Deut. 33:27). We have all the attributes of the Deity at our command.

Oh, Christian, when God says He always looks at you, He means that He is always yours. There is nothing that you need that He will refuse to do. There is no wisdom stored up in Him that He will not use for you. God will not withhold even one attribute of all of His great splendor, but all that God is will be yours. He will be your God forever and ever (Ps. 48:14). He will give you grace and glory (Ps. 84:11), and He will be your guide even unto death (Ps. 48:14).

YOUR GOD

Perhaps the sweetest term of the text is that next one—the eyes of Jehovah "thy God" (Deut. 11:12). Ah, there is a blessed secret! Why? He is ours in covenant, our God, for He has chosen us to be His portion, and by His grace He has made us choose Him to be our portion. We are His, and He is ours.

So I my best Beloved's am,
So he is mine.

"Thy God." Blessed be the Lord, we have learned to view Him not as another man's God, but as our God. Christian, can you claim God as yours this day? Has your hand by faith grasped Him? Has your heart by love twisted its tendrils around Him? Do you feel that He is the greatest possession that you have, that all else is but a dream, an empty show, but that God is your substantial treasure, your All in All?

Oh, then it is not an absolute God whose eyes are upon you, but God in covenant relationship who regards you. "Thy God." What a term this is! He who is watching me is my Shepherd. He who cares for me is my Father. He is not my God by way of power alone, but my Father by way of relationship.

He is so great that the heaven of heavens cannot contain Him, yet He deigned to visit this poor earth robed in mortal flesh. And He is now our God, the God of His people by near and dear relationship. In ties of blood, Jesus is one with sinners—our Husband, our Head, our All in All. We are His fullness, "the fulness of him that filleth all in all" (Eph. 1:23).

Thus, the eyes of God, as the covenant God of Israel, are upon His people "from the beginning of the year even unto the end of the year" (Deut. 11:12).

Much more may be said about the words of this text, but it is better unsaid by me, if you let the text say it to you. Talk to the text, I pray you. Let it journey with you until you can say about it what the disciples said about Christ: "Did not our heart burn within us, while he talked with us by the way?" (Luke 24:32).

OUR EYES UPON GOD

We are now going to turn the text around. That is, we will misread it, yet read it rightly. Suppose the text were to go like this: "The eyes of the Lord's people are always upon Him from the beginning of the year to the end of the year." Dear friends, I like the text as it stands, but I do not believe we will ever comprehend its full meaning unless we read it this other way, for we only understand God's sight of us when we get a sight of Him. God, unknown to us, is our protector, but He is not such a protector that we can comfortably repose upon Him. We must discern Him by the eyes of faith, or else the mercy, though given by God, is not spiritually enjoyed in our hearts.

Beloved, if God looks at us, how much more ought we to look at Him! When God sees us, what does He see? If He were to look at us in ourselves, He would see nothing but that which is unworthy to be looked at. (I praise God that He sees us in Christ!) Now, on the contrary, when we look at Him, what do we see? Oh, such a sight that I am not surprised that Moses said, "I beseech thee, show me thy glory" (Exod. 33:18). What a vision it is! Is it not a vision of heaven itself to see God? Is it not the prerogative of the pure in heart that they will see God (Matt. 5:8)?

Yet, I cannot figure something out. Some of us have had the right to see God for years, and we have occasionally seen Him face to face, "as a man speaketh unto his friend" (Exod. 33:11). By faith we have seen God. But, beloved, what I cannot figure out is why we see Him so little. Do you ever find yourself living all day without God? Not perhaps completely, for you would not want to go to work without a little prayer in the morning. But, do you not sometimes get through that morning's prayer without seeing God at all? I mean, is it not just the form of kneeling down and saying good words and getting up again? And all through the day have you not lived away from God?

This is a strange world to live in; there are not many things to make us happy. Yet, somehow we forget the very things that could give us happiness, and we keep our eyes on the frivolous cares and teasing troubles, which distract us.

So, do we even end the day with no taste of His love, no kisses from His lips, which are "better than wine" (Song 1:2)? And our evening prayer—poor moaning that it is—is hardly a prayer.

I fear it is possible to live not only days, but months at this dying rate, and it is horrible living. I would infinitely prefer to rot in a moldy dungeon and have the Lord's presence, than to live in the noblest palace without God. After all, that which makes life life is the enjoyment of the presence of God.

It is not so with the worldling: he can live without God. He is like the swine, who, being contented with their husks, lie down and sleep and wake again to feed. But, the Christian cannot live on husks, for he has a stomach above them. If he does not get his God, he is miserable.

God has ordained that a spiritual man is wretched without the love of God in his heart. If you and I want present happiness without God, we had better be sinners outright and feed on this world, rather than trying to be happy in religion without communion with Jesus. For a genuine Christian, happiness apart from Christ is an absolute impossibility. We must have God, or "we are of all men most miserable" (1 Cor. 15:19).

Suppose that this year we were filled with the desire to have our eyes always upon God from the beginning of the year to the end of the year, to be always conscious that He is seeing us, to be always sensible of His presence. More than that, suppose that this year we were always longing to be obedient to His commands, always wanting to win souls for His dear Son, from the beginning of the year to the end of the year. What a happy thing this would be! If we could abide in a spirit of prayerfulness and thankfulness—devout, consecrated, loving, and tender—it would be a high thing to attain.

Friends, we believe in a great God who "is able to do exceeding abundantly above all that we ask or think" (Eph. 3:20). Why not expect great things from Him? If I think of a blessing and dare to ask for it, surely then He is able to give it. Let us not stand back because of unbelief; let us ask that as God's eyes are upon us, our eyes may be upon Him. What a blessed meeting of eyes when the Lord looks us full in the face, and we look at Him through the mediator Christ Jesus, and the Lord declares, "I love you," and we answer, "We also love You, O our God!"

Oh, that we may be in harmony with the Lord our God and find ourselves drawn upwards and bound to Him! May the Lord be the sun and we the dewdrops that sparkle in His rays and are evaporated and drawn upward by the heat of His love! May God look down from heaven, and we look up to heaven, and both of us be happy in the sight of each other, delighting and rejoicing in mutual affection! This is what communion means. I have taken a long time to come to that definition, but that is what it means.

> Daily communion let me prove
> With thee, blest object of my love.

That was Toplady's desire. If I would express my own experience, I must close with the other two lines of the verse, where Toplady said,

> But oh, for this no strength have I,
> My strength is at thy feet to lie.

A WORLD WITHOUT GOD'S WATCHFUL CARE

In the third place, we will, in our imaginations, blot the text out altogether. Not that we could blot it out or would do so if we could. But, suppose for a moment that it is blotted out of the Bible. Imagine that you and I have to live all year without the eyes of God upon us, not finding a moment from the beginning of the year to the end of the year in which we perceive the Lord to be caring for us. Imagine that there is no one to whom we may appeal for help except our own fellowman.

Oh, miserable supposition! We would have to get through the year somehow. We would go muddling through the winter, groaning through the spring, sweating through the summer, fainting through the autumn, and groveling on through another winter. Imagine having no God to help us, no prayer because God is gone, no promise because God is no more. There could be no promise, no comfort, no spiritual help for us if there were no God. But, I hear you cry out, "Do not imagine such a thing, for I would be like a child without a father. I would be help-less—a tree with no water for its roots."

But I *will* imagine this in the case of you sinners. You know you have been living for twenty or thirty or forty years without God, without prayer, without trust, without hope. Yet, if I were to tell you solemnly that God would not let you pray during the next year, and would not help you if you did pray, you would be greatly startled. Although I believe that the Lord will hear you from the beginning of the year to the end of the year, although I believe that He will watch over you and bless you if you seek Him, yet I fear that most of you are despising His care and living without fel-lowship with Him. So, you are without God, without Christ, without hope, and will con-tinue to be from the beginning of the year to the end of the year.

Power in the Blood

There is a story about a most eccentric minister. Walking outside one morning, he saw a man going to work and said to him, "What a lovely morning! How grateful we ought to be to God for all His mercies!" The man said he did not know much about God's mercies. "Why," said the minister, "I suppose you always pray to God for your wife and children, don't you?"

"No," he said, "I do not know that I do."

"What," said the minister, "do you never pray?"

"No."

"Then I will give you ten dollars if you will promise me you will never pray as long as you live."

"Oh," he said, "I will be very glad for ten dollars to get me some beer."

He took the money and promised never to pray as long as he lived. He went to work, and when he had been digging for a little while, he thought to himself, "That's a strange thing I have done this morning—a very strange thing. I've taken money and promised never to pray as long as I live." He thought it over, and it made him feel wretched. He went home to his wife and told her about it.

"Well, John," she said, "you may count on it that it was the Devil. You've sold yourself to the Devil for ten dollars." This so weighed the poor wretch down that he did not know what

96

to do with himself. All he could think about was
that he had sold himself to the Devil for money
and would soon be carried off to hell. He started
to attend places of worship, believing that it was
of no use, for he had sold himself to the Devil.
He was really ill, bodily ill, because of the fear
and trembling that had come upon him.

One night at church, the sick man recognized the preacher. He was the very man who
had given him the ten dollars! The preacher
probably recognized him, for the text was,
"What shall it profit a man, if he shall gain the
whole world, and lose his own soul?" (Mark
8:36). The preacher remarked that he knew a
man who had sold his soul for ten dollars. The
poor man rushed forward and said, "Take it
back! Take it back!"

"You said you would never pray," said the
minister, "if I gave you ten dollars. Do you want
to pray?"

"Oh, yes, I would give the world to be al-
lowed to pray."

That man was a great fool to sell his soul
for ten dollars. But, some of you are even bigger
fools, for no one gave you ten dollars, and yet
you do not pray. I dare say you never will, but
you will go down to hell having never sought
God.

Perhaps, if I could say the opposite of this
text to you—"the eyes of God will not be upon

you from the beginning of this year to the end of this year, and God will not hear and bless you"—it might alarm and awaken you. But, though I suggest the thought, I long for you to say, "Oh, let not such a curse rest on me, for I may die this year, and I may die this day. O God, hear me now!" Ah, dear reader, if such a desire is in your heart, the Lord will hear you and bless you with His salvation.

OUR RESPONSE TO GOD'S PROMISE

Let us close by using the text for a practical lesson. The way to use it is by answering this question: If the eyes of the Lord will be upon us His people, from the beginning of the year to the end of the year, what should we be doing? Why, let us be as happy as we can during this year. Trials and troubles will come; do not expect to be free from them. The Devil is not dead, and sparks still fly upward (Job 5:7). Herein is your joy: the God and Father of our Lord Jesus Christ will never leave you nor forsake you (Heb. 13:5). Up with your flag now, and march on boldly! In the name of the Lord, set up your banner, and begin to sing. Away with burdensome care; God cares for us (1 Pet. 5:7). God feeds the sparrows; will He not feed His children (Matt. 6:26)? God clothes the lilies; will He not clothe the saints (Matt. 6:28–30)?

Let us roll all our burdens upon the Burden-bearer.

You will have enough to care for if you care for His cause as you should. Do not spoil your power to care for God by caring for yourself. This year let your motto be, "Seek ye first the kingdom of God, and his righteousness; and all these things shall be added unto you" (Matt. 6:33). By worrying you can neither add a cubit to your stature (Matt. 6:27), nor turn one hair white or black (Matt. 5:36). "Take therefore no [anxious] thought for the morrow: for the morrow shall take thought for the things of itself" (Matt. 6:34). Lean upon your God, and remember His promise: "As thy days, so shall thy strength be" (Deut. 33:25).

The apostle said, "I would have you without carefulness" (1 Cor. 7:32). He does not mean, "I do not want you to use economy, prudence, or discretion," but he means, "I do not want you to have fretfulness or distrustful care. I do not want you to be concerned for yourself, because the Lord's eyes will be upon you."

Furthermore, dear friends, I would have you use the text to seek greater blessings and richer mercies than you have ever enjoyed. Blessed be God for His merciful kindness towards His church. His loving-kindnesses have been very many. His favors are new every morning (Lam. 3:22–23) and fresh every even-ing. However, we want more. Let us not be content to wait until we have revival services to get a blessing; let us seek that blessing today.

I hope you Sunday school workers will be blessed. I hope the Sunday school classes will be blessed from the beginning of the year to the end of the year. Let there be no dullness, lethargy, and lukewarmness in our Sunday school classes. Let our teachers speak with fervor and earnestness: there must be no coldness in our classrooms. And I hope you who are preaching in the streets or going from house to house with tracts, or doing anything else, will have a blessing as you do so.

Will we grow cold as the year progresses? Not at all. We will serve God from the beginning of the year to the end of the year. Will we endeavor to get up a little excitement and have a revival for five or six weeks? No, blessed be God, we must have revival from the beginning of the year to the end of the year. Since we have a spring of water that never grows dry (Isa. 58:11), why should the pitcher ever be empty? Surely, gratitude can find us fuel enough in the forests of memory to keep the fire of love always flaming. Why should we be weary when the glorious prize is worthy of our constant exertions, when the great crowd of witnesses keeps us in its sight (Heb. 12:1)?

May our Lord by His Spirit bring you and me to a high pitch of prayerfulness, and then let us continue in prayer from the beginning of the year to the end of the year. May God bring you and me to a high degree of generosity. Then, may we always be giving from the beginning of the year to the end of the year, every week from the first to the last, always giving money for His cause as God has prospered us (1 Cor. 16:2). May we be always active, always industrious, always hopeful, always spiritual, always heavenly, and always raised up and made to "sit together in heavenly places in Christ Jesus" (Eph. 2:6).

May God deal graciously with us from the beginning of the year to the end of the year through Jesus Christ our Lord. Amen.

4

A Tempted Savior—
Our Best Help

For in that he himself hath
suffered being tempted, he is able to
succour them that are tempted.
—Hebrews 2:18

One important area in which God helps us from the beginning of the year to the end of the year is that of temptation. Recently, a friend of mine, who is a clergyman of the Church of England, wrote to me and included this verse about temptation, Hebrews 2:18. This man is a venerable clergyman, who has always shown me the most constant and affectionate regard. This text is dear to this aged servant of the Lord because of his deep experience of both affliction and deliverance. Through these experiences he has learned his need of solid, substantial food, fit for the veteran warriors of the cross. Having been tempted these many years, my friend finds that as his natural strength decays, he needs to cast himself more and more upon the tenderness of the Redeemer's love. And he is led to look more fully to Him who is his only help in the day of trouble, finding consolation alone in the person of Christ Jesus the Lord.

Hebrews 2:18 is a staff for old age to lean on in the rough places of the way. It is a sword with which the strong man may fight in all hours of conflict. It is a shield with which youth may cover itself in the time of peril. And it is a royal chariot in which spiritual babes may ride in safety. There is something here for every one of us, as Solomon put it: "A portion to seven, and also to eight" (Eccl. 11:2). If we consider the Great Prophet and High Priest of our profession—Jesus Christ—as being tempted in all points (Heb. 4:15), we will not grow weary or faint in our minds. No, we will prepare to run in our future journey, and like Elijah we will go in the strength of this meat for many days to come (1 Kings 19:8).

You that are tempted—and I suppose most readers would fall into this category—read what I have tried to explain about your temptations and the temptations of Jesus. For Jesus, having known your trials, is able to help you at all times.

CHRIST WAS TEMPTED

Our first point is this: many souls are tempted—even Christ was tempted. All the heirs of heaven have carried this burden. All true gold must feel the fire. All wheat must be threshed. All diamonds must be cut. All saints must endure temptation.

Saints are tempted from every direction. It is like Christ's parable about the house built on the rock. The Bible says,

> *The rain descended, and the floods came, and the winds blew, and beat upon that house; and it fell not: for it was founded upon a rock.* (Matt. 7:25)

The descending rain may represent temptations from above. The floods pouring their devastating torrents over the land may denote the trials that spring from the world. And the howling winds may typify those mysterious influences of evil that issue from the "prince of the power of the air" (Eph. 2:2).

Now, whether we shudder at the descending rain, fear the uprising flood, or are amazed at the mysterious energy of the winds, we should remember that our blessed Lord "was in all points tempted like as we are" (Heb. 4:15). This is to be our consolation: nothing has happened to the members of Christ's body that has not happened to Christ, the Head.

Tempted by God

Beloved friends, it is possible that we may be tempted by God. I know it is written that "God cannot be tempted with evil, neither tempteth he any man" (James 1:13). Yet, I read in Scripture, "It came to pass...that God did tempt Abraham" (Gen. 22:1). Also, part of the prayer that we are taught to offer before God is, "Lead us not into temptation" (Matt. 6:13). This verse clearly implies that God does lead into temptation, or why else would we be taught to entreat Him not to do so?

In one sense of the term *tempt,* a pure and holy God can have no share, but in another sense He does tempt His people. The temptation that comes from God is altogether that of trial. God's trials are not meant for evil like Satan's temptations, but they are trials meant to prove and strengthen our graces. All at once, God's trials illustrate the power of divine grace, test the genuineness of our virtues, and strengthen our character.

You remember that Abraham was tried and tested by God when he was bidden to go to a mountain that God would show him, there to offer up his son Isaac. (See Genesis 22:1–2.)

You and I may have a similar experience. God may call us in the path of obedience to a great and singular sacrifice. The desire of our eyes may be demanded of us in an hour. Or, He may summon us to a duty far surpassing all our strength; and we may be tempted by the weight of the responsibility, like Jonah, to flee from the presence of the Lord (Jonah 1:3).

We do not know which temptations we will face until we come to them; but, beloved, whatever they may be, our Great High Priest has felt them all. His Father called Him to a work of the most terrific kind. He "laid on him the iniquity of us all" (Isa. 53:6). He ordained Him as the second Adam, the bearer of the curse, the destroyer of death, and the conqueror of hell. Jesus was the seed of the woman, doomed to be wounded in the heel but elected to bruise the Serpent's head (Gen. 3:15). Our Lord was appointed to toil at the loom, and there, with ever-flying shuttle, to weave a perfect garment of righteousness for all His people (Isa. 61:10).

Now, beloved, this was a strong and mighty testing of Jesus' character. It is impossible that we could ever be thrust into a refiner's fire as hot as the one that tried this purest gold. No one else could be in the crucible so long or subjected to a heat so hot as that which was endured by Christ Jesus. If, then, the trial is sent directly from our heavenly Father, we may solace ourselves with this reflection: "In that [Christ] himself hath suffered being tempted [of God], he is able to succour them that are [likewise] tempted" (Heb. 2:18).

But, dear friends, our God tries us not only directly, but indirectly. Everything is under the Lord's control of providence. Everything that happens to us is meted out by His decree and settled by His purpose. We know that nothing can happen to us unless it is written in the secret book of providential predestination. Consequently, all the trials resulting from circumstances can be traced at once to the great First Cause. Out of the golden gate of God's ordinance, the armies of trial march forth in array. No shower falls from the threatening cloud unless God permits it; every drop has its orders before it hastens to the earth.

Consider poverty, for instance. So many people are made to feel its pinching necessities. They shiver in the cold for lack of clothes. They are hungry and thirsty. They are homeless, friendless, despised. This is a temptation from God, but Christ suffered the same: "Foxes have holes, and the birds of the air have nests; but the Son of man hath not where to lay his head" (Matt. 8:20). When He had

A Tempted Savior—Our Best Help

fasted forty days and forty nights, He was
hungry, and it was then that He was tempted
of the Devil. (See Matthew 4:2–3.)

It is not only the scant table and the rag-
ged garment that invite temptation, for all
providences are doors to trial. Even our mercies, like roses, have their thorns. Men may be
drowned in seas of prosperity as well as in rivers of affliction. Our mountains are not too
high, and our valleys are not too low, for temptation to travel. Where can we go to get away
from temptations? What wind is strong
enough to carry us away from them? Everywhere, above and beneath, we are troubled
and surrounded by dangers. Now, since all
these trials are overseen and directed by the
great Lord of providence, we may look at them
all as temptations that come from Him.

Christ suffered every kind of temptation.
Let us choose the special one of sickness. Sickness is a strong temptation to impatience, re-
bellion, and murmuring, but He "Himself took
our infirmities, and bare our sicknesses"
(Matt. 8:17). His appearance was marred more
than that of any man (Isa. 52:14) because His
soul was sorely vexed and, consequently, His
body was greatly tormented.

Bereavement, too, is such a trial to the
tender heart! You arrows of death, you kill,
but you wound with wounds worse than death.

"Jesus wept" (John 11:35) because His friend
Lazarus slept in the tomb. That great loss
taught Jesus to sympathize with the widow in
her loss, with the orphan in his fatherless estate, and with the friend whose acquaintance
has been thrust into darkness. Nothing can
come from God to the sons of men unless the
same thing or a similar thing also happened to
the Lord Jesus Christ. Herein let us wrap the
warm cloak of consolation around ourselves,
since Christ was tempted like we are.

Tempted by Men

We are tempted more often by men than
by God. God tries us now and then, but our
fellowmen every day. Our foes are in our own
household and among our own friends. Out of
mistaken kindness, they would often lead us to
prefer our own ease to the service of God.
Links of love have made chains of iron for
saints. It is hard to ride to heaven over our
own flesh and blood. Relatives and acquaintances may greatly hinder the young disciple.

This, however, is no novelty to our Lord.
You know how He had to say to Peter, well-
beloved disciple though he was, "Get thee behind me, Satan...thou savourest not the things
that be of God" (Matt. 16:23). Poor, ignorant
human friendship tried to keep Jesus back

from the cross. It would have made Him miss His great purpose for being fashioned as a man, and it would have robbed Him of all the honor that only shame and death could win Him.

Not only true friends, but also false friends attempt our ruin. Treason creeps like a snake in the grass; and falsehood, like an adder, bites the horse's heels (Gen. 49:17). If treachery assaults us, let us remember how Jesus was betrayed: "He that eateth bread with me hath lifted up his heel against me" (John 13:18). "Yea, mine own familiar friend, in whom I trusted, which did eat of my bread, hath lifted up his heel against me" (Ps. 41:9). What should be done to you, false tongue? Eternal silence rest on you! And yet, you have spent your venom on my Lord; why should I marvel if you try your worst on me?

We are tempted by friends, and we are often assailed by enemies. Enemies will waylay us with subtle questions, seeking to trap us by our words. Oh, cunning devices of a generation of vipers! They did the same to Christ. The Sadducee, the Pharisee, the lawyer—each one had his riddle. And each one was answered—answered gloriously—by the Great Teacher, who cannot be trapped.

You and I are sometimes asked strange questions. Doctrines are set in controversy with other doctrines. Texts of Scripture are made to clash with other texts of Scripture. We hardly know how to reply to these things. Let us retire into the secret chamber of this great fact: in this point, also, Christ was tempted.

When Jesus' foes could not prevail against Him with questions, they slandered His character. They called Him "a man gluttonous, and a winebibber, a friend of publicans and sinners" (Matt. 11:19). He became the song of the drunkard, and their reproach broke His heart.

This may happen to us. People may accuse us of the very thing of which we are the most innocent. Our good deeds may be misrepresented, our motives misinterpreted, our words misreported, and our actions misconstrued. In this, also, we may shelter ourselves beneath the eagle wings of this great truth: our glorious Head has suffered, and, having been tempted, He can give us aid.

However, His foes did even more than this. When they found Him in an agony of pain, they taunted Him to his face (Matt. 27:39–40). Pointing with the finger, they mocked His nakedness. Thrusting out the tongue, they jeered at His claims. They hissed out that diabolical temptation: "If he be the King of Israel, let him now come down from the cross, and we will believe him" (Matt. 27:42).

How often the sons of men have mocked us and then accused us in like manner. They have caught us in some unhappy moment— when our spirits were broken, when our circumstances were unhappy—and then they have said, "Now where is your God? If you are what you profess to be, prove it." They ask us to prove our faith by a sinful action, which they know would destroy our characters— some rash deed that would be contrary to our profession of faith. Here, too, we may remember that, having been tempted, our High Priest is able to help those who are tempted.

Moreover, remember that there are temptations that come from neither friends nor foes, but from those with whom we are compelled to mix in ordinary society. Jesus ate at a Pharisee's table, even though most Pharisees reeked with infectious pride. He sat with the publicans, even though their characters were contagious with impurity. But, whether it was in one difficult place or another, the Great Physician walked through the midst of moral plagues and leprosies unharmed. He associated with sinners but was not a sinner. He touched disease but was not diseased Himself. He could enter into the chambers of evil, but evil could not find a chamber in Him.

You and I are thrown by our daily duties into constant contact with evil. It is impossible,

I suppose, to walk among men without being tempted by them. Men who have no preconceived plan to betray us, entice us to evil and corrupt our good manners simply by the force of their ordinary behavior. We may cry, "Woe is me, that I sojourn in Mesech, that I dwell in the tents of Kedar!" (Ps. 120:5). However, we may remember that our great Leader sojourned here, too; and being here, He was tempted even as we are (Heb. 4:15).

Tempted by Satan

Dear friends, we will not complete the list of temptations if we forget that a vast host, and those of a most violent nature, can only be ascribed to satanic influence. Satan's temptations are usually threefold, for Christ's threefold temptation in the wilderness, if I read it right, was a true picture of all the temptations that Satan uses against God's people. The first temptation of Satan is usually made against our faith. When our Lord was hungry, Satan came to Him and said, "If thou be the Son of God, command that these stones be made bread" (Matt. 4:3). Here it was, that devilish "if," that cunning suggestion that He was not God's Son, coupled with the enticement to commit a selfish act to prove that He was the Son.

Ah, how often Satan tempts us to unbelief! "God has forsaken you," he says. "God has no love for you. Your experience has been a delusion. Your profession of faith is a falsehood. All your hopes will fail you. You are only a poor, miserable fool. There is no truth in religion. If there is, why are you in this trouble? Why not do as you like, live as you want, and enjoy yourself?" Ah, foul fiend, how craftily you spread your net, but it is all in vain, for Jesus has passed through and broken the snare.

Dear reader, beware of intermeddling with divine providence. Satan tempts many believers to run before the guiding cloud, to carve their own fortunes, to build their own houses, to steer their own ships. Trouble will surely befall all who yield to this temptation. Beware of becoming the keepers of your own souls, for evil will soon overtake you. Ah, when you are thus tempted by Satan and your adoption seems to be in jeopardy and your experience appears to melt, fly at once to the Good Shepherd. Remember this: "In that he himself hath suffered being tempted, he is able to succour them that are tempted" (Heb. 2:18).

The next foul temptation of Satan with Christ was not to unbelief, but to the very opposite—presumption. "Cast thyself down" (Matt. 4:6), he said, as he poised the Savior on the pinnacle of the temple. Even so, he whispers to some of us, "You are a child of God; you know that. Therefore, you are safe to live as you like. 'Cast thyself down from hence: For it is written, He shall give his angels charge over thee, to keep thee' (Luke 4:9–10)."

Oh, that foul temptation! It leads many an antinomian by the nose, and he is like "an ox [going] to the slaughter, or as a fool to the correction of the stocks" (Prov. 7:22). For many an antinomian will say, "I am safe; therefore, I may indulge my lusts with impunity."

You see, the Devil tries to use the doctrine of election or the great truth of the final perseverance of the saints to tempt you to soil your purity. He tries to use the mercy and love of God to tempt you to stain your innocency. However, you who know better, when you are thus tempted, console yourselves with the fact that Christ was tempted in this way, too, and He is able to help you even here.

The final temptation of Christ in the wilderness was that of idolatry. Actually, ambition was the temptation, but idolatry was the end at which the tempter aimed. "All these things will I give thee, if thou wilt fall down and worship me" (Matt. 4:9). The old Serpent will suggest to us, "I will make you rich if you will only venture upon that one dishonest transaction. You will be famous; only tell that one lie. You will be perfectly at ease; only wink at one small evil. All these things will I give you if you will make me lord of your heart." Ah, then it will be a noble thing if you can look up to Him who endured this temptation and bid the fiend depart with, "It is written, Thou shalt worship the Lord thy God, and him only shalt thou serve" (Matt. 4:10). Then, Satan will leave you, and angels will minister to you as they did to the tempted One of old.

Tempted in All Positions

Not only are we tempted from all directions, but we are tempted in all positions. No man is too lowly for the arrows of hell; no man is too elevated for the arrows of hell. Poverty has its dangers: "Lest I be poor, and steal" (Prov. 30:9). Christ knew these dangers. Contempt has its aggravated temptations. To be despised often makes men bitter; it often exasperates them into savage selfishness and wolfish revenge. Our Great Prophet knew from experience the temptations of contempt.

It is no small trial to be filled with pain. When all the strings of our personhood are strained and twisted, it is little wonder if they make a sour note. Christ endured the greatest amount of physical pain, especially upon the cross. And on the cross, where all the rivers of human agony met in one deep lake within His heart, He bore all that it was possible for the human frame to bear. Here, then, without limit, He learned the ills of pain.

Turn the picture around: Christ knew the temptations of riches. You may say, "How?" He had opportunities to be rich. Mary, Martha, and Lazarus would have been glad to give Him their substance. The honorable women who ministered to Him would have grudged Him nothing. There were many opportunities to make Himself a king. He could have become famous and great like other teachers and earned a high salary. However, knowing the temptations of wealth, He also overcame them.

The temptations of ease—and these are not small—Christ readily escaped. There always would have been a comfortable home for Him at Bethany. There were many disciples who would have felt highly honored to find for Him the softest couch ever made. But, He who came not to enjoy but to endure spurned all, but not without knowing the temptation.

He learned, too, the trials of honor, popularity, and applause. "Hosanna, hosanna, hosanna," said the multitudes in the streets of Jerusalem, as palm branches were strewn in the way and He rode in triumph over the garments of His disciples. (See Matthew 21:6–9.) But, experiencing all this, He was still meek and lowly, and in Him was no sin (1 Pet. 2:21–22).

When you are cast down or lifted up, when you are put into the strangest of positions, remember that Christ has made a pilgrimage over the least trodden of our paths and is therefore able to help them that are tempted.

Tempted at All Ages

Further, let me remark that every age has its temptations. Even children, if believers, will discover that there are peculiar snares for them. Christ knew these. It was no small temptation to a twelve-year-old boy to be found sitting in the midst of the doctors, hearing them and answering their questions. It would have caused pride in most boys, and yet Jesus went down to Nazareth and was subject to His parents (Luke 2:51).

It says in Luke 2:52 that "Jesus increased in wisdom and stature, and in favour with God and man." It would be dangerous to grow in favor with God and man if the word *God* were not included. To grow in favor constantly with men would be too much of a temptation for most teenagers. It is good for a man to bear the yoke in his youth; for youth, when honored and esteemed, is too apt to grow self-conceited, vain, and disobedient.

When a young man knows that he will become something great someday, it is not easy

to keep him balanced. Suppose that he is born
to an estate and knows that when he grows up
he will be lord and master and will be popular
with everybody. Why, he is apt to be very way-
ward and self-willed. Now, there were prophe-
cies that went before concerning Mary's son.
They pointed Him out as King of the Jews
(Matt. 2:1–2) and a mighty one in Israel. Yet, I
do not find that the holy child Jesus was ever
lured by His coming greatness into any evil actions. So, teenage believers, you who are like
Samuels and Timothys, you can look to Christ
and know that He can help you.

It is unnecessary for me to repeat the various afflictions that beat upon Jesus in His full
manhood. You who today bear the burden and
heat of the day will find an example here. Old
age, also, does not need to look elsewhere, for
we may view our Redeemer with admiration as
He went up to Jerusalem to die. His last moments were obviously near at hand; He knew
the temptations of an expected death. He saw
death more clearly than any of you, even if your
temples are covered with white hair. Yet,
whether in life or in death, on Tabor's summit
or on the banks of the river of death, He is still
the same—tempted ever, but never sinning;
tried always, but never found failing. O Lord,
You are able to help those who are tempted.
Help us!

I do not need to write more about this. Perhaps I have not mentioned your particular trial, but it may be included in one of the general descriptions. Whatever your trial may be, it cannot be so rare that it is not included somewhere in the temptations of our Lord Jesus Christ. I, therefore, now turn to the second topic of this chapter.

CHRIST SUFFERED

My second point is that as the tempted often suffer, Christ also suffered. Notice, our text does not say, "In that He Himself has also been tempted, He is able to help them that are tempted." It is better than that. The text tells us that Christ suffered: "In that he himself hath suffered being tempted, he is able to succour them that are tempted" (Heb. 2:18). Temptation, even when overcome, brings to the true child of God a great deal of suffering.

The Shock of Sin

This suffering consists of two or three things. It lies, mainly, in the shock that sin gives to the sensitive, regenerate nature. A man who is clothed in armor may walk through tearing thorns and brambles without being hurt; but if he takes off his armor and attempts the same journey, how sadly he will be cut and torn. Sin, to the man who is used to it, is no suffering. Being tempted causes him no pain. In fact, temptation frequently yields pleasure to the sinner. To look at the bait is sweet to the fish that plans to swallow it before long. But the child of God, who is spiritually new and alive, shudders at the very thought of sin. He cannot look at sin without abhorrence and without being alarmed at the possibility of falling into an abominable crime.

Now, dear friends, in this case Christ indeed has experience, and it far surpasses ours. His hatred of sin must have been much deeper than ours. A word of blasphemy, a sinful deed, must have cut Him to His very heart. We cannot even comprehend the wretchedness that Jesus must have endured in merely being on earth among the ungodly. For infinite purity to dwell among sinners must be something like the best educated, the most pure, the most amiable person being condemned to live in a den of burglars, blasphemers, and filthy wretches. That man's life would be misery. No whip or chain would be needed. Merely associating with such people would be pain and torment enough. So, the Lord Jesus must have suffered a vast amount of woe just by being near to sin.

The Dread of Temptation

Suffering, too, comes to the people of God from the dread of a temptation. Dread arises in our hearts as the shadow of the temptation falls upon us, announcing its soon arrival. At times there is more dread in the prospect of a trial than there is in the trial itself. We feel a thousand temptations in fearing one.

Christ knew this. What an awful dread came over Him in the black night of Gethsemane! It was not the cup—it was the fear of drinking it. He cried, "Let this cup pass from me" (Matt. 26:39). He knew how black, how foul, how fiery its contents were; and it was the dread of drinking it that bowed Him to the ground until He sweat, as it were, great drops of blood (Luke 22:44). When you have a similar overwhelming pressure on your spirit in the prospect of a trial, fly to the loving heart of your sympathizing Lord, for He has suffered all this.

The Source of Temptation

Temptation also causes suffering because of its source. Have you ever felt that you would not have minded the temptation if it had not come from where it did? "Oh," you say, "to think that my own friend, my dearly beloved friend, should tempt me!" Perhaps you are a teenager, and you have said, "I think I could bear anything but my father's frown or my mother's sneer." Perhaps you are a husband, and you have said, "My thorn in the flesh is too sharp, for it is an ungodly wife." Or, you are a wife (and this is more frequently the case), and you think there is no temptation like yours, because it is your husband who assaults your religion and who speaks evil of your good.

It makes all the difference where the temptation comes from. If some scoundrel mocks us, we think it honor; but when it is an honored companion, we feel his taunt. A friend can cut under our armor and stab us the more dangerously.

Ah, but the Man of Sorrows knew all this, since it was one of the chosen twelve who betrayed Him. Moreover, "it pleased the LORD to bruise him; he hath put him to grief" (Isa. 53:10). To find God to be in arms against us is a huge affliction. "Eloi, Eloi, lama sabachthani?...My God, my God, why hast thou forsaken me?" (Mark 15:34) is the very emphasis of woe. Jesus surely has suffered your griefs, regardless of their source.

The Fear of Dishonoring God

I have no doubt, too, that a portion of the suffering of temptation lies in the fact that

God's name and honor are often involved in our temptation. Those of us who are in the public eye are sometimes slandered. When the slander is merely against our own personal character, against our modes of speech or habit, we can receive it gratefully and thankfully, blessing God that He has counted us worthy to suffer for His name's sake (Acts 5:41). However, sometimes the attack is very plainly not against us, but against God. People say things that make us cry with the psalmist David, "Horror hath taken hold upon me because of the wicked that forsake thy law" (Ps. 119:53).

When direct blasphemies are uttered against the person of Christ, or against the doctrine of His holy Gospel, my heart has been very heavy because I have thought, "If I have opened this dog's mouth against myself, it does not matter; but if I have made him roar against God, then how will I answer, and what will I say?" This has often been the bitterness of it: "If I fall, God's cause is stained. If I slip through the vehemence of this assault, then one of the gates of the church will be carried off by storm. Harm comes not just to me, but to many of the Israel of God." David says this about grieving the saints: "When I thought to know this, it was too painful for me" (Ps. 73:16).

Power in the Blood

Jesus had to suffer for God, for it is written, "The reproaches of them that reproached thee fell on me" (Rom. 15:3). He was made the target for those arrows that were really shot at God, and so He felt this bitterness of sympathy with His ill-used God.

I cannot, of course, be specific enough to hit on the precise sorrow that you, beloved believer in Christ, are enduring as the result of temptation. But, whatever phase your sorrow may have assumed, this should always be your comfort: Jesus suffered in temptation. He did not merely know temptation as you sometimes have known it, when it has hit you and fallen harmless to the ground, but it festered in His flesh. It did not make Him sin, but it made Him suffer. It did not make Him err, but it caused Him to mourn. Oh, child of God, I do not know a deeper well of purer consolation than this: "He himself hath suffered being tempted" (Heb. 2:18).

CHRIST HELPS THE TEMPTED

Now for the third and last point. Those who are tempted have great need of help; and Christ, having been tempted Himself, is able to help them. Of course, Christ is able to help the tempted because Christ is God. Even if He had never endured any temptation, He would

126

still be able to help the tempted because He is God. However, we are now speaking in our text of Christ as a high priest; we are to regard Him in His complex character as God-man. For Christ is not only God, but man, and not only man, but God. The *Christos,* the Anointed One, the High Priest of our profession, is, in His complex character, able to help them that are tempted.

Because He Was Tempted

How can He help us? Why, first, the very fact that He was tempted has help in it for us. If we had to walk through the darkness alone, we would know the very extremity of misery. But, having a companion, we have comfort; having such a companion, we have joy.

Darkness surrounds me, and the path is miry, and I sink in it and can find no foothold. But, I plunge onward, desperately set on reaching my journey's end. It worries me that I am alone. I can see nothing, but suddenly I hear a voice that says, "Yea, though I walk through the valley of the shadow of death, I will fear no evil" (Ps. 23:4). I cry out, "Who is there?" and an answer comes back to me: "I, 'the faithful and true witness' (Rev. 3:14), the 'Alpha and Omega' (Rev. 1:8), the sufferer who was 'despised and rejected of men' (Isa.

53:3), I lead the way." Then, at once, light surrounds me, and there is a rock beneath my
feet. If Christ my Lord has been here, then the
way must be safe and must lead to the desired
end. The very fact that He has suffered, then,
consoles His people.

Because He Was Not Destroyed

But, further, the fact that He has suffered
without being destroyed is inestimably comforting to us. Think about a block of ore just
ready to be put into the furnace. Suppose that
block of ore could look into the flames and could
see the blast as it blows the coals to a vehement
heat. If that ore could speak, it would say, "Ah,
how awful that I should ever be put into such a
blazing furnace as that! I will be burnt up! I will
be melted with the slag! I will be utterly con-
sumed!" But, suppose another lump all bright
and glistening could lie by its side and say, "No,
no, you are just like I was, but I went through
the fire and lost nothing. See how bright I am!
See how I have survived all the flames!" Why,
that piece of ore would anticipate, rather than
dread, being exposed to the purifying heat. It
would anticipate coming out all bright and lus-
trous like its companion.

I see You, Son of Mary, bone of our bone,
flesh of our flesh (Gen. 2:23). You have felt the

flames, but You are not destroyed. There is no smell of fire on You. Your heel has been bruised, but You have broken the Serpent's head (Gen. 3:15). There is no scar, nor spot, nor injury in You. You have survived the conflict. Therefore, I, bearing Your name, purchased with Your blood (Acts 20:28), and as dear to God as You are dear to Him, I will survive the conflict, too. I will tread the coals with confidence and bear the heat with patience. Christ's conquest gives me comfort, for I will conquer, too.

Because He Was a Great Gainer

Please remember, too, that Christ, in going through the suffering of temptation, not only did not lose anything, but He gained much. Through suffering, He was a great gainer. It is written that it pleased God "to make the captain of their salvation perfect through sufferings" (Heb. 2:10). It was through His suffering that He obtained the mediatory glory that now crowns His head. If He had never carried the cross, He would have never worn that crown. (It is a transcendently bright and glorious crown that He now wears as King in Zion and as leader of His people, whom He has redeemed by blood.) Had He not carried the cross, He would still have been God over all and blessed forever; however, He could never have been extolled as the God-man Mediator unless He had been obedient even unto death (Phil. 2:8). Therefore, He was a gainer by His suffering.

Glory be to His name, we get comfort from this, too! For we also will be gainers by our temptations. We will come up out of Egypt enriched, as it is written, "He brought them forth also with silver and gold" (Ps. 105:37). We will come forth out of our trials with great treasures. "Blessed is the man that endureth temptation: for when he is tried, he shall receive the crown of life" (James 1:12). The deeper our sorrows, the louder our song. The more terrible our toil, the sweeter our rest. The more bitter the wormwood, the more delightful the wine of consolation. We will have glory for our shame; we will have honor for our contempt; we will have songs for our sufferings; and we will have thrones for our tribulations.

Because He Sends His Grace to Help Us

Moreover, because Christ has suffered temptation, He is able to help us who are tempted by sending His grace to help us. He was always able to send grace; but now as God and man, He is able to send just the right grace at the right time and in the right place. A doctor may have all the drugs that can be gathered, but an abundance of medicine does not make him a qualified practitioner. If, however, he has gone himself and seen the case, then he knows just at what crisis of the disease a certain medicine is needed. The medications are good, but the wisdom to use the medications— this is even more precious.

Now, "it pleased the Father that in [Christ] should all fulness dwell" (Col. 1:19). But, where would the Son of Man earn His diploma and gain the skills to use the fullness correctly? Beloved, He won it by experience. He knows what sore temptations mean, for He has felt the same. You know, if we had comforting grace given to us at the wrong point in our temptation, it would tempt us more than help us. It is just like certain medicines: given to the patient at one period of the disease, they would worsen the malady, though the same medicine would cure him if administered a little later.

Now, Christ knows how to send His comfort in the nick of time. He gives His help exactly when it will not be a superfluity. He sends His joy when we will not spend it upon our own lusts. How does He do this? Why, He recollects His own experience; He has passed through it all. "There appeared an angel unto him from heaven, strengthening him" (Luke

22:43). That angel came just when he was needed. Jesus knows when to send His angelic messenger to strengthen you, when to use the correcting rod, and when to refrain and say, "I have forgiven you. Go in peace."

Because He Prays for Us

I will not write much more on this subject. Having suffered Himself, having been tempted, Christ knows how to help us by His prayers for us. There are some people whose prayers are of no use to us because they do not know what to ask for. Christ is the intercessor for His people; He has success in His intercession; but how does He know what to ask for? How can He know this better than by His own trials? He has suffered temptation.

You hear some believers pray with such power, such unction, such fervor. Why? Part of the reason is that they pray from experience— they pray out of their own lives; they just tell the great deep waters over which they themselves sail. Now, the prayer of our Great High Priest in heaven is wonderfully comprehensive. It is drawn from His own life, and it takes in every sorrow and every pang that ever rent a human heart, because He Himself has suffered temptation. I know you feel safe in committing your case into the hand of such an intercessor, for He knows the precise mercy for which to ask. And, when He asks for it, He knows how to word it so that the mercy will surely come at the right time.

Ah, dear friends, it is not in my power to bring out the depth that lies in my text. However, I am certain of this: when He causes you to go through the deep waters, when you are made to pass through furnace after furnace, you will never need a better support or provision than my text: "In that he himself hath suffered being tempted, he is able to succour them that are tempted" (Heb. 2:18). Hang this text up in your house; read it every day; take it before God in prayer every time you bend your knee. You will find it to be like the widow's cruse of oil, which did not go dry, and like her handful of meal, which did not run out (1 Kings 17:16). It will sustain you as much a year from now as it does when you begin to feed on it today.

Will my text not suit the awakened sinner as well as the saint? Perhaps you are a timid soul that cannot say that you are saved. Yet, here is a loophole of comfort for you, you poor troubled one who is not yet able to get a hold of Jesus: "He is able to succour them that are tempted" (Heb. 2:18). Go and tell Him you are tempted—tempted, perhaps, to despair, tempted to self-destruction, tempted to go back to your old sins, tempted to think that Christ cannot save you. Go and tell Him that He Himself has suffered temptation and that He is able to help you. Believe that He will, and He will, for you can never believe in the love and goodness of my Lord too much. He will be better than your faith to you. If you can trust Him with all your heart to save you, He will do it. If you believe He is able to put away your sin, He will do it. Only honor Him by attributing to Him a good character of grace; you cannot give Him too good a name.

> Trust him, he will not deceive you,
>   Though you hardly on him lean;
> He will never, never leave you,
>   Nor will let you quite leave him.

Receive, then, the blessing. May the grace of our Lord Jesus Christ, the love of God our Father, and the fellowship of the Holy Spirit be with you forever. Amen and Amen.

5

True Unity Promoted

*Endeavouring to keep the unity of the Spirit
in the bond of peace.*
—Ephesians 4:3

The people of the church are often tempted to spread strife and division. I hope this verse, Ephesians 4:3, will be useful to us all. It will remind us of our former faults and of our present duty in the matter of "endeavouring to keep the unity of the Spirit in the bond of peace."

In former days, when some of the churches of Christ began to shake the yoke of popedom from their necks, the argument used against reformation was the necessity of maintaining unity. The argument went something like this: "You must bear with this ceremony and that dogma, no matter how anti-Christian and unholy it is. You must endeavor 'to keep the unity of the Spirit in the bond of peace'

135

(Eph. 4:3)." That is what the old Serpent said in those early days. And the argument continued like this: "The church is one; woe to those who create division! It does not matter that Mary is set up in the place of Christ, that images are worshiped, that rotten rags are adored, and that pardons for every kind of crime are bought and sold. It does not matter that the so-called church has become an abomination and a nuisance on the face of the earth. Still, you must 'keep the unity of the Spirit in the bond of peace.' You must lie down, restrain the testimony of the Spirit of God within you, keep His truth under a bushel, and let the lie prevail." This was the grand reasoning of the Church of Rome.

Believers, there is no force in this argument if you will look at the text for a moment. The text tells us to endeavor to keep the unity of the *Spirit,* but it does not tell us to maintain the unity of evil or the unity of superstition. The unity of error, false doctrine, and priests' schemes may have in it the spirit of Satan—we do not doubt it—but it is not the unity of the Spirit of God. We are to break down the unity of evil by every weapon that our hands can grasp. It is the unity of the Spirit that we are to maintain and foster.

Remember, we are forbidden to do evil that good may come (Rom. 3:8). The following things are evil: restraining the witness of the Spirit of God within us, concealing any truth that we have learned by the revelation of God, and holding back from testifying for God's truth against the sin and folly of man's inventions. This is sin of the blackest hue.

We dare not commit the sin of quenching the Holy Spirit (1 Thess. 5:19), even if we are trying to promote unity. The unity of the Spirit never requires any support of sin. This unity is maintained, not by suppressing truth, but by publishing it abroad. One of the pillars of the unity of the Spirit is witnessing about the one faith that God has revealed in His Word. This unity is quite different from the "unity" that would gag our mouths and turn us all into dumb, driven cattle, to be fed or slaughtered at the will of priestly masters.

Dr. McNeil has, very properly, said that a man can scarcely be an earnest Christian in the present day without being a controversialist. We are sent forth today "as sheep in the midst of wolves" (Matt. 10:16); can we have agreement with wolves? We are like lamps in the midst of darkness; can we have harmony with darkness (2 Cor. 6:14)? Did not Christ Himself say, "Think not that I am come to send peace on earth: I came not to send peace, but a sword" (Matt. 10:34)? You can understand how all this controversy is the truest method of trying to keep the unity of the Spirit; for Christ, the Man of War, is Jesus the Peacemaker. In order to create lasting, spiritual peace, the concord of evil must be broken, and the unity of darkness must be dashed to pieces.

I pray that God will always preserve us from a unity in which truth is considered valueless, in which principle gives place to policy, in which the masculine virtues of the Christian hero are supplemented by an effeminate, fake love. May the Lord deliver us from indifference to His Word and will, for this creates a cold unity—like masses of ice frozen into an iceberg, chilling the air for miles around; or like the unity of the dead as they sleep in their graves, contending for nothing because they no longer have a part in the land of the living.

There is a unity that is seldom broken: the unity of devils, who, under the service of their evil master, never disagree and quarrel. From this terrible unity keep us, O God of heaven! There is the unity of locusts, who have one common object: the glutting of themselves to the ruin of all around. From this unity, also, save us, we pray! There is the unity of the waves of hell's fire, sweeping myriads into deeper misery. From this, also, O King of heaven, save us evermore!

May God perpetually send some prophet who will cry aloud to the world: "Your covenant with death shall be disannulled, and your agreement with hell shall not stand" (Isa. 28:18). May there always be found some men, though they are as rough as Amos, or as stern as Haggai, who will denounce again and again all league with error and all compromise with sin. May they declare that these evil alliances and compromises are abhorred by God.

Never dream that holy contention is a violation of Ephesians 4:3: "Endeavouring to keep the unity of the Spirit in the bond of peace." We must destroy every union that is not based on truth before we can enjoy the unity of the Spirit. We must first sweep away these walls of untempered mortar—these tottering fences of man's building—before there can be room to lay the strong stones of Jerusalem's walls. It is these walls that will bring lasting prosperity. I have written these things in order to clear a path to reach my text.

Three things are clear from the text: first, there is a unity of the Spirit to be kept; second, it needs keeping; and third, a bond is to be used. When I have expounded on these points, I will give practical applications of the text, first to Christians in their connection with other churches, and then to members of

the same church in their connection with
each other.

A UNITY WORTH KEEPING

First, there is a unity of the Spirit that is
worthy to be kept. You will notice that it is not
an ecclesiastical unity; it is not endeavoring to
keep the unity of the denomination, the com-
munity, the diocese, or the parish. No, it is
"endeavouring to keep the unity of the Spirit"
(Eph. 4:3). Men speak of the Episcopal church,
the Wesleyan church, or the Presbyterian
church. Now, I do not hesitate to say that
there is nothing whatsoever in Scripture that
is even similar to such language, for there I
read of the seven churches in Asia (Rev. 1:4):
the church in Corinth, Philippi, Antioch, and
so on.

In England there are thousands of
churches adhering to the episcopal form of
government; in Scotland there are thousands
of churches adhering to the presbyterian form
of government; among the Wesleyans there are
churches adhering to Mr. Wesley's form of
government. However, to speak of a whole
cluster of churches as one church is not in accordance with Scripture, but only in accordance with human invention. Although I
myself am inclined to a presbyterian union

among our churches, I cannot help perceiving in Holy Scripture that each church is separate and distinct from every other church. All of them are connected by those various bonds and ligaments that keep all the separate churches together, but they are not so connected that they run into each another and lose their separateness and individuality. There is nothing in Scripture that says, "Endeavoring to keep up your ecclesiastical arrangements for centralization." No, the exhortation goes like this: "Endeavouring to keep the unity of the Spirit" (Eph. 4:3).

Again, you will observe that it does not say, "Endeavoring to keep the uniformity of the Spirit." The Spirit does not recognize uniformity. Take nature, for instance. The flowers are not all tinted with the same hue, nor do they give off the same odors. There is variety everywhere in the work of God. If I glance at providence, I do not perceive that any two events happen the same way; the page of history is varied.

If, therefore, I look at the church of God, I do not expect to find that all Christians speak the same way or see with the same eyes. We rejoice to recognize that there is "one Lord, one faith, one baptism, one God and Father of all" (Eph. 4:5–6). But, as for uniformity in dress, liturgical verbiage, or form of worship, I find nothing of it in Scripture. Men may pray acceptably standing, sitting, kneeling, or lying with their faces to the ground. They may meet with Jesus by the river's side, in a church, in a prison, or in a house. They may be one in the same Spirit although "one man esteemeth one day above another: [and] another esteemeth every day alike" (Rom. 14:5).

What, then, is this unity of the Spirit? I trust, dear friends, that we know it by possessing it, for it is certain that we cannot *keep* the unity of the Spirit if we do not have it already. Let us ask ourselves the question, "Do we have the unity of the Spirit?" The only ones that can have it are those who have the Spirit, and the Spirit dwells only in born-again, believing souls. By virtue of his having the Spirit, the believer is in union with every other spiritual man, and this is the unity that he is to endeavor to keep.

This unity of the Spirit is manifested in love. A husband and wife may be, through providence, cast hundreds of miles from one another, but there is a unity of spirit in them because their hearts are one. I am divided many thousands of miles from the saints in Australia, Africa, and the South Seas; but, loving them as brothers, I feel the unity of the Spirit with them. I have never attended a church meeting in Africa; I have never worshiped God with the Samoans or with my brothers in New Zealand; but, notwithstanding, I feel the unity of the Spirit in my soul with them, and everything that concerns their spiritual welfare is important to me.

This unity of the Spirit is caused by a similarity of nature. You may find a drop of water glittering in the rainbow, leaping in the waterfall, rippling in the stream, lying silent in the stagnant pool, or spraying against the ship's side. Each one of these drops of water claims kinship with every drop of water the whole world over, because it is the same in its elements. Similarly, there is a unity of the Spirit that we cannot fake. It consists of these things: being "begotten...again unto a lively hope by the resurrection of Jesus Christ from the dead" (1 Pet. 1:3), bearing in us the Holy Spirit as our daily quickener, and walking in the path of faith in the living God. Here is the unity of spirit; it is a unity of life, nature working itself out in love. This is sustained daily by the Spirit of God. He who makes us one, keeps us one.

Every member of my body must have communion with every other member of my body. I say *must*. As far as I know, the members of my body never ask each other whether they will be in harmony or not. As long as there is life in my body, every separate portion

of my body must have communion with every
other portion of it. Take, for example, my finger. Imagine that I discolor it with some noxious drug. My head may not approve of the
staining of my finger, and my head may suggest a thousand ways to clean that finger.
However, my head never says, "I will cut off
that finger." My tongue speaks loudly against
the noxious fluid that has blistered my finger
and caused pain to my entire body. Yet, my
tongue cannot say, "I will have that finger cut
off," unless my body is willing to be forever
mutilated and incomplete.

Now, it is impossible to mutilate the body
of Christ. Christ does not lose His members or
cast off parts of His body. Therefore, a Christian should never ask himself whether he
should have communion in spirit with a certain Christian, for he cannot do without it. As
long as he lives, he must have it. This does not
stop him from boldly denouncing the error
into which his brother may have fallen, or
from avoiding his intimate acquaintance while
he continues to sin. However, we can never
really sever any true believer from Christ, or
from ourselves if we are in Christ Jesus.

The unity of the Spirit is preserved, then,
by the Holy Spirit's infusing life daily into the
one body. As the life become stronger, that
union becomes more manifest. Let a spirit of

prayer be poured out on all our churches—
then conventionalities will be dashed down;
divisions will be forgotten; and, arm in arm,
the people of God will show to the world that
they are one in Christ Jesus. (See Galatians
3:28.)

There are some activities during which
this unity of the Spirit is certain to show itself.
One is prayer. How truly Montgomery put it:

> The saints in prayer appear as one
> In word, and deed, and mind,
> While with the Father and the Son,
> Sweet fellowship they find.

There is a unity of praise, too. Our hymn
books differ very little after all. We still sing
the same song, the praise of the same Savior.
Then, there is a unity of working together: we
have a union in our conflict with the common
foe, and in our contention for the common
truth. This leads to communion. I do not mean
sitting down to the same table to eat bread and
drink wine; that is only the outward union. I
mean the communion in which many hearts
beat as one and there is a feeling that we are
all one in Christ Jesus.

Bucer's motto was to love everyone in
whom he could see anything of Christ Jesus.
Let this be your motto, too, fellow believer. Do

not make your love an excuse for not offering stern rebuke, but rebuke because you love. Some people think that unless you cover your words with sugar, unless you cringe and compliment and conceal, there is no love in your heart. But, I trust it will be our privilege to show that we can sternly disapprove and yet love; that we can shun our brother's error and yet, in our very shunning, prove our affection to him, and to our common Master.

It is said of some men that they were born on the mountains of Bether, for they do nothing but cause division, or that they were baptized in the waters of Meribah, for they delight in causing strife. (See Exodus 17:7.) This is not the case with the genuine Christian; he cares only for the truth, for his Master, for the love of souls. When these things are not in danger, his own private likes or dislikes never hinder his communion with other Christians. He loves to see another church prosper as much as his own. As long as he knows that Christ is glorified, it does not matter to him which minister God uses, where souls are converted, or what form of worship is used.

Yet, the genuine Christian always holds to this: there is no unity of the Spirit where there is a lie involved. Where the souls of men are concerned, he would be a traitor to God if he did not witness against the damning error and testify for the saving truth. Where the crown jewels of his Master's kingdom are concerned, he dares not traitorously hold his tongue. No, though his fellow subjects throw his name out as evil, he counts it all joy, as long as he is faithful to his Master and obeys his conscience as before "the Judge of [the] quick and dead" (Acts 10:42).

KEEPING THE UNITY

Now that we know that there is a unity of the Spirit worthy to be kept, I want to point out that it needs to be kept. It is a very difficult thing to maintain, for several reasons. First of all, our sins would, very naturally, break it. If we were all angels, we would keep the unity of the Spirit and not even need the exhortation to do so. But, alas, we are proud, and pride is the mother of division. Diotrephes, who loves to have preeminence (3 John 1:9), is very sure to head a faction. How envy, too, has separated good friends! When I cannot be satisfied with anything that is not hammered on my workbench, when another man's candle grieves me because it gives more light than mine, and when another man troubles me because he has more grace than I have—oh, there is no unity in this case. Anger—what a deadly foe that is to unity! When we cannot overlook the smallest disrespect, when the slightest thing turns our faces red, when we speak unadvisedly with our lips—surely then there is no unity. But, I do not need to read the long list of sins that spoil the unity of the Spirit, for it is lengthy. Oh, may God cast them out of us, for only then can we keep the unity of the Spirit.

But, beloved, our very virtues may make it difficult for us to keep this unity. Luther was brave and bold, hot and impetuous; he was just the man to clear the way for the Reformation. Calvin was logical, clear, cool, precise; he seldom spoke rashly. It was not natural for Luther and Calvin to always agree. Their very virtues caused them to argue. Consequently, Luther, in a bad temper, called Calvin a pig and a devil. And, although Calvin once replied, "Luther may call me what he will, but I will always call him a dear servant of Christ," yet John Calvin knew how to pierce Luther under the fifth rib when he was angry.

In those days the courtesies of Christians to one another were generally of the iron glove kind, rather than the naked hand. They were all called to war for the sake of the truth, and they were so intent on their task that they were even suspicious of their fellow soldiers. It may be the same way with us: the very watchfulness of truth, which is so valuable, may make us suspicious where there is no need for suspicion. And, our courage may take us where we should not go, like a fiery horse that carries a young warrior beyond where he intended to go, where he may be taken prisoner. We must watch—the best of us must watch—lest we fight the Lord's battles with Satan's weapons and thereby, even from love to God and His truth, violate the unity of the Spirit.

The unity of the Spirit ought to be kept, dear friends, because Satan is so busy trying to mar it. He knows that the greatest glory of Christ will spring from the unity of His church.

> *That they all may be one; as thou, Father, art in me, and I in thee, that they also may be one in us: that the world may believe that thou hast sent me.*
> *(John 17:21)*

There is no church happiness where there is no church unity. If a church is divided, the schism is death to all sacred fellowship. We cannot enjoy communion with each other unless our hearts are one. How feeble is our work for God when we are not in agreement!

The enemy cannot desire a better ally than strife in the midst of our camp. "Can you not agree," said a warrior of old, "when your enemy is in sight!" Christians, can you not agree to

keep the unity of the Spirit when a destroying
Satan is ever on the watch, seeking to drag
immortal souls down to perdition? (See 1 Peter
5:8.) We must be more diligent in this matter.
We must purge ourselves of everything that
would divide us, and we must equip our hearts
with every holy thought that would unite us.
When I join a Christian church, I should not
say, "I am sure I will never break this church's
unity." I am to suspect myself of tending to-
ward that evil, and I am to watch with all dili-
gence that I keep the unity of the Spirit.

THE BOND OF PEACE

I have now come to my third point. In order to keep the unity of the Spirit, there is a
bond provided—the bond of peace. Beloved,
there should be much peace, perfect peace, and
unbounded peace among the people of God. We
are not strangers; we are "fellowcitizens with
the saints, and of the household of God" (Eph.
2:19). Realize your fellow citizenship, and do
not treat Christian people as foreigners; then
this common bond of citizenship will be a bond
of peace.

Men may be fellow citizens and still be
enemies, but you are friends. You are all
friends to Christ, and in Him you are all
friends to one another. Let that be another

bond. But, your relationship goes even deeper. You are not just friends, you are brothers, born of the same Parent, filled with the same life. Will this not bind you together? "See that ye fall not out by the way" (Gen. 45:24). Do not contend with one another, for you are brothers. (See Acts 7:26.)

But, this is not all. You are even closer than brothers, for you are members of the same body! Will this mysterious union fail to be a bond of peace to you? Will you, being the foot, contend with the eye? Or, will you, being the eye, contend with the hand and say, "I have no need of you" (1 Cor. 12:21)? The joints and bones in a person's body do not disagree. If it is really true that we are members of Christ's body, let it never be said that the various parts of Christ's body would not work together but instead battled one another. What a monstrous thing to be said!

I believe I have brought out the meaning of the text. There is a unity of the Spirit that is worthy to be kept. We ought to keep it. We must try to keep it in the bond of peace.

PRACTICAL CONCLUSIONS

Now I will come to the practical conclusions of the subject—first, in the connection of one church with another, and, second, in the connection of one church member with another.

Church to Church

It is not a desirable thing for all churches to melt into one another and become one. The complete fusion of all churches into one ecclesiastical corporation would inevitably produce another form of popery, since history teaches us that large ecclesiastical bodies grow more or less corrupt as a matter of course. Huge spiritual corporations are, as a whole, the strongholds of tyranny and the refuges of abuse; and it is only a matter of time until they will break into pieces. Disruption and secession must occur, and will occur, where a unity is attempted that is not meant in God's Word.

However, it will be a blessed thing when all the churches walk together in the unity of the Spirit. What a wonderful thing when that church over there, although it baptizes its members and laments the neglect of that ordinance by other churches, yet feels that the unity of the Spirit must not be broken and holds out its right hand to all who love our Lord Jesus Christ in sincerity. What a refreshing thing when this church over here, governed by its elders, feels a unity with another church that is presided over by its bishop. What an

inspiring thing when a certain church that believes in mutual edification and no ministry, is
yet not quarrelsome towards those who love
the ministry of the Word.

What a great thing when churches have
agreed about this one thing: we will search the
Word independently and act out, according to
our light, what we find to be true. Having done
so, we will "keep the unity of the Spirit in the
bond of peace" (Eph. 4:3). Yes, these things
are most desirable; we should seek after them.
We should not seek to fuse all churches into
one denomination, but we should seek to keep
each distinct church in love with every other
church.

Now, in order to do this, I have a few sug-
gestions to offer. It is quite certain we will
never keep the unity of the Spirit if each
church declares that it is superior to every
other. If there is a church that says, "We are
the church, and all others are mere sects; we
are established, and others are only tolerated,"
then it is a troublemaker and must hide its
head when the unity of the Spirit is so much
as hinted at. Any church that lifts up its head
and boasts over other churches has violated
the unity of the Spirit. On the other hand, if a
group of churches says, "One church is our
master, and we are all brothers," they do not
violate the unity of the Spirit, for they simply

claim their rights and speak the truth. The church that forgets its true position as one in the family and begins to set itself up as master and claim preeminence over its fellow servants, has put it out of its own power to keep the unity of the Spirit, for it has violated it once and for all.

Again, a church that wants to keep the unity of the Spirit must not consider itself to be so infallible that not to belong to its membership is sin. What right has any one church to set itself up as the standard, so that those who do not join it are dissenters? It is true my Episcopal brother is a dissenter, for he dissents from me; it is true he is a nonconformist, for he does not conform to me. I would not, however, call him by such names, lest I should arrogantly imply that my own church is *the* church, and so break the unity of the Spirit.

You may believe that your church can claim a long line of ancestors descending from the apostles, without ever running through the Church of Rome, but should you therefore call a brother who does not quite see this succession, a schismatic, and call his assembly a cult? If he is a schismatic because he does not go to your church, why are you not a schismatic because you do not go to his? You say, "Well, but, he divides the church! He ought to come and worship with me." Ought you not to go and worship with him? You say, "Ah, but there are more of us!" Are divine things to be ruled by the majority? Where would the church of God be if it came to polling? I am afraid the Devil would always be at the head of the poll. We wish to keep the unity of the Spirit, and if we have a smaller sister church, we will treat her all the more kindly, owing to the fewness of her members.

If I want to "keep the unity of the Spirit in the bond of peace" (Eph. 4:3), I must never call in the magistrate to force my brother to pay my church so that it can buy choir robes, ring the church bell, and keep the building clean. I must not tell my brother that he is bound to pay for the support of my worship. If I do, he will say, "Oh, my dear friend, I pay for the maintenance of the worship that I believe to be correct, and I am quite willing that you should do the same for yours. I would voluntarily assist you if you were poor, but you tell me you will put me in prison if I do not pay, and yet you tell me to keep the unity of the Spirit. My dear friend, it is not keeping the unity of the Spirit to take away my stool and my table and my candlestick, and say you will put me in jail or drag me before an ecclesiastical court. You send the police after me; and then if I say a word about it, you say, '[Love] hopeth all things' (1 Cor. 13:7). Yes, among the rest, it hopes that you will give up your sin in this matter."

If we should own of a piece of ground where we bury our dead, and if there should happen to come a member of another Christian church who would wish to lay his poor dead baby in our ground, there being no other convenient spot anywhere, and he asks the favor, I think we can hardly be thought of as keeping the unity of the Spirit if we tell him, "No, nothing of the kind. You had your child sprinkled; therefore, it cannot be buried with us Christians. We will not have your sprinkled baby lying alongside our baptized dead." I do not think that is keeping the unity of the Spirit. When some churches have sent away from their graveyard gate the mourners who have brought an unbaptized infant, and the mourners have gone back weeping to their homes, I do not think such churches have been "endeavouring to keep the unity of the Spirit in the bond of peace" (Eph. 4:3).

Again, if churches are to agree with one another, they must not make rules that ministers who are not of their own denomination cannot occupy their pulpits. I should be ashamed if my congregation would pass a resolution that no one dissenting from us could stand in my pulpit. But, we know a church that says, "We will not allow in our pulpit any minister who is not of our denomination, no matter how good a man he may be. He may be a man as venerated as John Angell James or have all the excellencies of a William Jay, and we would not, perhaps, mind hearing him in a town hall, but into the sacredness of our particular pulpit these intruders must not come. For we have ministers; you have only lay teachers. We have the sacraments; the cup of blessing that we bless is the blood of Christ, and the bread that we break is the body of Christ. You have no sacramental power with you; you are not a church, but only a body of schismatics, meeting together to carry out what you think to be right. We tolerate you; that is all we can do." Where is the unity of the Spirit there?

It is wrong for any church to stand up and say, "We are *the* church; our ministers are *the* ministers; our people are *the* people. Now, dear brothers, shake hands, and endeavor to keep the unity of the Spirit of God." Why, it is preposterous! Let us meet on equal ground; let us lay aside all pretenses to superiority; let us really aid and not oppress each other; let us mingle in prayer; let us unite in confession of sin; let us join heartily in reforming our errors; and a true evangelical alliance will cover our land.

If any church will take the Bible as its standard, and in the power of the Spirit of God preach the name of Jesus, there are thousands of us who will rejoice to give them the right hand of fellowship. We are every day striving to get other churches and ourselves more and more into that condition in which, while holding our own, we can yet keep the unity of the Spirit in the bond of peace.

Church Member to Church Member

Now I will write a few words to you in regard to your relationship to one another as members of the same church. If we are to endeavor "to keep the unity of the Spirit in the bond of peace" (Eph. 4:3) in the same church, then we must avoid everything that would mar it. Gossip is a very ready means of separating friends from one another. Let us endeavor to talk of something better than each other's characters.

Dionysius went down to Plato's academy, and Plato asked what he came for. "Why," said Dionysius, "I thought that you, Plato, would be talking against me to your students." Plato answered, "Do you think, Dionysius, we are so destitute of matter to discuss that we talk about you?" Truly, we must be very short of subjects when we begin to talk of one another. It is far better to magnify Christ than detract from the honor of His members.

We must lay aside all envy. Multitudes of good people liked the Reformation, but they said they did not like that it was done by a poor miserable monk like Martin Luther. So there are many who like to see good things done, but they do not care to see it done by that young, upstart brother or that poor man or woman who has no particular rank. As a church, let us shake off envyings; let us all rejoice in God's light.

As for pride, if any of you have grown vainglorious lately, shake it off. I hope to have a ministry that will drive out those who will not acknowledge their brothers when they are poorer or less educated than themselves. So what if a person mars the English language when he talks? What does that matter, as long as his heart is right? As long as you can feel he loves the Master, surely you can put up with his faults of speech, if he can put up with your faults of action.

Let us cultivate everything that would tend to unity. Are any sick? Let us care for them. Are any suffering? Let us weep with them. Do we know someone who has less love than others? Then let us have more to make up the deficiency. Do we perceive faults in a brother? Let us admonish him in love and affection. I implore you to be peacemakers, everyone. Let the church go on in holy accord and blessed unity.

Let us remember that we cannot keep the unity of the Spirit unless we all believe the truth of God. Let us search our Bibles, therefore, and conform our views and sentiments to the teaching of God's Word. I have already told you that unity in error is unity in ruin. We want unity in the truth of God through the Spirit of God. Let us seek after this; let us live near to Christ, for this is the best way of promoting unity.

Divisions in churches never begin with those full of love for the Savior. Cold hearts, unholy lives, inconsistent actions, neglected prayer closets—these are the seeds that sow schisms in the body. However, he who lives near to Jesus, wears His likeness, and copies His example, will be, wherever he goes, a sacred bond, a holy link, to bind the church together more closely than ever. May God give us this, and from now on let us endeavor "to keep the unity of the Spirit in the bond of peace" (Eph. 4:3).

I commend the text to all believers to be practiced throughout the coming year. And, those of you who are not believers, I trust your unity and your peace may be broken forever, and that you may be led to Christ Jesus to find peace in His death. May faith be given to you, and then love and every grace will follow, so that you may be one with the church of Christ Jesus our Lord. Amen.

6

Creation's Groans and Saints' Sighs

For we know that the whole creation groaneth and travaileth in pain together until now. And not only they, but ourselves also, which have the firstfruits of the Spirit, even we ourselves groan within ourselves, waiting for the adoption, to wit, the redemption of our body.
—Romans 8:22–23

Our sighs should never come from having a disunited church. But, even if the church is perfectly united, we will still have other reasons to sigh. Our text, Romans 8:22–23, attests to this. Unfortunately, this text is far from easy to handle. The more I read it, the more I am certain that this is one of the things to which Peter referred when he wrote about Paul's epistles and said, "In which are some things hard to be understood" (2 Pet. 3:16). However, dear friends, we have often found that the nuts that are hardest to crack have the sweetest kernels, and the bones that are hardest to break have the richest marrow. So it may be with this text; so it will be if the Spirit of God is our instructor, for He will fulfill His gracious promise to "guide [us] into all truth" (John 16:13).

The whole creation is fair and beautiful even in its present condition. I have no sympathy with those who cannot enjoy the beauties of nature. Climbing the lofty Alps, wandering through the charming valley, skimming the blue sea, or walking through the green forest, I have felt that this world, however desecrated by sin, was built to be a temple of God; and the grandeur and the glory of it plainly declare that "the earth is the LORD'S, and the fulness thereof" (Ps. 24:1). Like the marvelous structures of Palmyra of Baalbek, the earth in ruins reveals a magnificence that speaks of a royal founder and an extraordinary purpose.

Creation glows with a thousand beauties, even in its present fallen condition; yet, clearly, it is not the same as when it came from the Maker's hand. The slime of the Serpent is on it all, and this is not the world that God pronounced to be "very good" (Gen. 1:31). We hear of tornadoes, earthquakes, tempests, volcanoes, avalanches, and the sea that kills thousands; there is sorrow on the sea, and there is misery on the land. Into the highest palaces as well as the poorest cottages, Death, the insatiable, is shooting his arrows, while his quiver is still full to bursting with future woes.

It is a sad, sad world. The curse has fallen on it since the Fall, and it brings forth thorns and thistles. Earth wears on her brow, like Cain of long ago, the brand of transgression. (See Genesis 4:15.) It would be sad to think that this were always to be so. If there were no future for this world, as well as for ourselves, we would be glad to escape from this world, considering it nothing better than a huge prison from which we long to be freed.

At this present time, the groaning and travailing that are prevalent throughout creation, are deeply felt among the sons of men. The dreariest thing you can read is the newspaper. I heard of a person who sat up at the end of last year to groan last year out; he was not good at groaning, from what I hear, but in truth it was a year of groaning, and the present one opens amid turbulence and distress. We heard of abundant harvests, but we soon discovered that they were all a dream and that there would be scarcity in the worker's home. And now, what with conflicts between men and masters, which are banishing trade from England, and what with political convulsions, which unhinge everything, the ship of the state is drifting fast to shipwreck. May God in His mercy put His hand to the helm of the ship and steer her safely. There is a general wail among nations and peoples. You can hear it in the streets of the city. If we did not know that "the LORD reigneth" (1 Chron. 16:31), we might lament bitterly.

Our text tells us that not only is there a groan from creation, but this is shared by God's people. We notice in our text, first, what the saints have already attained; second, where they are deficient; and third, what the saints' state of mind is in regard to the whole matter.

WHAT THE SAINTS HAVE ALREADY ATTAINED

Before we were saved, we were an undistinguished part of the creation, subject to the same curse as the rest of the world, "children of wrath, even as others" (Eph. 2:3). But, distinguishing grace has made a difference where no difference naturally was; we are now no longer treated as criminals condemned, but as children and heirs of God (Rom. 8:16–17). We have received a divine life, by which we are made "partakers of the divine nature, having escaped the corruption that is in the world through lust" (2 Pet. 1:4). The Spirit of God has come to us so that our bodies are the temples of the Holy Spirit (1 Cor. 6:19). God dwells in us, and we are one with Christ.

We have in us at this present moment certain priceless things that distinguish us as believers in Christ from all the rest of God's creatures. "[We] *have* the firstfruits of the Spirit" (Rom. 8:23, italics added), not "we hope and trust we have," or "possibly we may have," but "we have, we know we have, and we are sure we have." Believing in Jesus, we speak confidently; we have unspeakable blessings given to us by the Father of spirits. Not we *will have,* but *we have.* True, many things are yet in the future, but even at this present moment "we have obtained an inheritance" (Eph. 1:11); we already have in our possession a divine heritage that is the beginning of our eternal portion.

This divine heritage is called "the firstfruits of the Spirit" (Rom. 8:23), which I understand to mean the first works of the Spirit in our souls. Beloved, we have repentance, that first gem of the Spirit. We have faith, that priceless, precious jewel. We have hope, which sparkles, a hope most sure and steadfast. We have love, which sweetens all the rest. We have that work of the Spirit within our souls that always comes before admittance into glory. We are already made new creatures in Christ Jesus (2 Cor. 5:17) by the effective working of the mighty power of God the Holy Spirit.

These are called the firstfruits because they come first. They are like the first sheaf of the harvest, which was waved before the Lord:

> *Speak unto the children of Israel, and say unto them, When ye be come into the land which I give unto you, and shall reap the harvest thereof, then ye shall bring a sheaf of the firstfruits of your harvest unto the priest: And he shall wave the sheaf before the LORD, to be accepted for you: on the morrow after the sabbath the priest shall wave it.*
> *(Lev. 23:10–11)*

Our spiritual lives are similar to this first sheaf, for all the graces that adorn the spiritual life are the first gifts, the first operations of the Spirit of God in our souls.

It is called firstfruits, again, because the firstfruits were always the pledge of the harvest. As soon as the Israelite had plucked the first handful of ripe ears, they were proof to him that the harvest was already come. He looked forward with glad anticipation to the time when the wagon would creak beneath the sheaves, and when "Harvest home" would be shouted at the door of the barn. So, beloved, when God gives us "faith, hope, charity, these three" (1 Cor. 13:13), when He gives us "whatsoever things are pure...lovely...of good report" (Phil. 4:8), as the work of the Holy Spirit, these are to us the forerunners of the coming glory. If you have the Spirit of God in your soul, you may rejoice over it as the pledge and token of the fullness of bliss and perfection "which God hath prepared for them that love him" (1 Cor. 2:9).

It is called firstfruits, again, because these were always holy to the Lord. The first ears of corn were offered to the Most High, and surely our new nature, with all its powers, must be regarded by us as a consecrated thing. The new life that God has given to us is not ours, that we should ascribe its excellence to our own merit; the new nature comes only from Christ. Since it is Christ's image and Christ's creation, so it is for Christ's glory alone. That new nature we must keep separate from all earthly things; that treasure that He has committed to us we must watch both night and day against those profane intruders who would defile the consecrated ground. We must stand on our watchtower and cry aloud to our strong Lord for strength (1 Chron. 16:11), that the adversary may be repelled, that the sacred castle of our hearts may be for the habitation of Jesus, and Jesus alone. We have a sacred secret that belongs to Jesus, as the firstfruits belong to Jehovah.

Beloved, the work of the Spirit is called firstfruits because the firstfruits were not the harvest. No Jew was ever content with the firstfruits. He was glad to have the firstfruits, but they enlarged his desires for the harvest. If he had taken the firstfruits home and said, "I have all I want," and had rested satisfied month after month, he would have proved that he was mad, for the firstfruits only whet the appetite—only stir up the desire that they cannot satisfy by themselves.

Therefore, when we get the first works of the Spirit of God, we are not to say, "I have attained my goal; I am already perfect; there is nothing further for me to do or to desire." No, my beloved, everything that the most advanced of God's people know now, should excite in them an insatiable thirst for more. My brother with great experience, my sister with a close friendship with Christ, you have not yet known the harvest; you have only reaped the first handful of corn. Open your mouth wide, and God will fill it (Ps. 81:10)! Enlarge your expectations, seek great things from the God of heaven, and He will give them to you. Do not, by any means, fold your arms in sloth and sit down on the bed of carnal security. Forget the steps you have already trodden, and reach forward towards that which is before (Phil. 3:13), "looking unto Jesus" (Heb. 12:2).

Even this first point, about the saint receiving only the firstfruits of the Spirit, will help us understand why he groans. As I have already stated, we have not received all of our portion. In fact, what we have received is to the whole no more than one handful of wheat is to the whole harvest—a very gracious pledge, but nothing more. Therefore, we groan. Having received something, we desire more. Having reaped handfuls, we long for sheaves. It is because of this very fact, the fact that we are saved, that we groan for something beyond.

Did you hear that groan just now? It is a traveler lost in the deep snow on the mountain pass. No one has come to rescue him, and indeed he has fallen into a place from which escape is impossible. The snow is numbing his limbs, and his soul is breathed out with many a groan. Keep that groan in your ear, for I want you to hear another.

Suppose the traveler has been rescued and taken to the lodge. He has been hospitably received; he has warmed himself at the fire; he has received abundant provision; he is warmly clothed. There is no fear of storm; that grand old lodge has outlasted many a thundering storm. The man is perfectly safe, and quite content, so far as that goes, and exceedingly grateful to think that he has been rescued.

Yet, I hear him groan because he has a wife and children on the plain down below, and the snow is too deep to travel in, and the wind is howling, and the blinding snowflakes are falling so thickly that he cannot pursue his journey. Ask him whether he is happy and content. He says, "Yes, I am happy and grateful. I have been saved from the snow. I do not wish for anything more than I have here; I am perfectly satisfied, so far as this goes. But, I long to see my family and to be once more in my own sweet home. And until I reach it, I will not stop groaning."

Now, the first groan that you heard was deep and dreadful, as though it were fetched from the abyss of hell; that is the groan of the ungodly man as he perishes and leaves all his dear delights. But, the second groan is so soft and sweet that it is rather the note of desire than of distress. Such is the groan of the believer, who, though rescued and brought into the lodge of divine mercy, is longing to see his Father's face without a veil between, and to be united with the happy family on the other side of the Jordan, where they will rejoice forevermore.

When the soldiers of Godfrey of Bouillon came in sight of Jerusalem, it is said they shouted for joy at the sight of the holy city. For that very reason they also began to groan. Do you ask why? It was because they longed to enter it. Having once looked upon the city of David, they longed to take the holy city by storm, to overthrow the crescent and place the cross in its place. He who has never seen the New Jerusalem has never clapped his hands with holy ecstasy; he has never sighed with the unutterable longing that is expressed in words like these:

> O my sweet home, Jerusalem,
>   Would God I were in thee!
> Would God my woes were at an end,
>   Thy joys that I might see!

I will give another illustration to show that the obtaining of something makes us groan after more. An exile, far away from his native country, has been long forgotten, but suddenly a ship brings him the pardon of his king and gifts from his friends who have remembered him. As he turns over each of these tokens of love, and as he reads the words of his reconciled prince, he asks, "When will the ship sail to take me back to my native shore?" If the ship waits, he groans over the delay; and if the voyage is tedious and adverse winds toss the ship, his longing for his own sweet land compels him to groan.

It is the same way with your children when they look forward to their holidays; they are not unhappy or dissatisfied with school, yet they long to be at home. Do you remember how, in your school days, you used to make a little calendar with a square for every day, and how you always crossed off the day as soon as it began, as though you were trying to make the time pass as quickly as possible? You groaned for it, not with the unhappy groan that marks one who is going to perish, but with the groan of one who, having tasted of the sweets of home, is not content until he can feast on them again.

So you see, beloved, it is because we have the firstfruits of the Spirit that we groan. We cannot help but groan for that blissful period that is called "the adoption, to wit, the redemption of our body" (Rom. 8:23).

WHAT THE SAINTS ARE LACKING

I now come to my second point, which is what the saints are lacking. We are deficient in those things for which we groan and wait. And there appear to be at least four of them.

Our New Bodies

The first is that these bodies of ours are not delivered. Beloved, as soon as a man believes in Christ, he is no longer under the curse of the law. (See Galatians 3:13.) As to his spirit, sin has no more dominion over him, and the law has no further claims against him. His soul is translated from death to life. But, the body, this poor flesh and blood, does it not remain as before? Not in one sense, for the members of our bodies, which were instruments of unrighteousness, become by sanctification the instruments of righteousness to the glory of God. (See Romans 6:13.) The body that was once a workshop for Satan becomes a temple for the Holy Spirit, wherein He dwells (1 Cor. 6:19).

However, we are all perfectly aware that the grace of God makes no change in the body in other respects. It is just as subject to sickness as before; pain throbs quite as sharply in the heart of the saint as in the heart of the sinner; and he who lives near to God is no more likely to enjoy bodily health than he who lives at a distance from Him. The greatest piety cannot preserve a man from growing old; although in grace he may be like a young cedar, fresh and green, yet the body will have its gray hairs, and the strong man will be brought to totter on the cane. The body is still subject to the evils that Paul mentioned when he said that it is subject to corruption, dishonor, and weakness, and is still a natural body. (See 1 Corinthians 15:42–44.)

These are not little things, for the body has a depressing effect on the soul. A man may be full of faith and joy spiritually, but I would challenge him to feel the same way under the ill effects of some diseases. The soul is like an eagle, and the body is like a chain that prevents its mounting. Moreover, the appetites of the body have a natural affinity to that which is sinful. The natural desires of the human frame are not in themselves sinful, but through the degeneracy of our nature, they very readily lead us into sin. Through the corruption that is in us, even the natural desires of the body become a very great source of temptation. The body is redeemed with the precious blood of Christ; it is redeemed by price; but it has not as yet been redeemed by power. It still lingers in the realm of bondage and is not brought into "the glorious liberty of the children of God" (Rom. 8:21).

Now, this is the cause of our groaning and mourning, for the soul is so married to the body that when it is itself delivered from condemnation, it sighs to think that its poor friend, the body, is still under the yoke. Suppose that you were a free man who had married a slave. You could not feel perfectly content; but the more you enjoyed the sweets of freedom yourself, the more you would mourn that she was still in slavery. So is it with the spirit: it is free from corruption and death, but the poor body is still under the bondage of corruption, and therefore the soul groans until the body itself is set free.

Will it ever be set free? Oh, my beloved, do not ask that question. This is the Christian's brightest hope. Many believers make a mistake when they long to die and go to heaven. That may be desirable, but it is not the ultimate satisfaction for the saints. The saints in heaven are perfectly free from sin, and, so far as they are capable of it, they are perfectly happy; but a disembodied spirit can never be perfect until it is reunited to its body. God made man not pure spirit, but body and spirit, and the spirit alone will never be content until it sees its physical body raised to its own condition of holiness and glory. Do not think that our longings here below are not shared by the saints in heaven. They do not groan because of any pain, but they long with greater intensity than you and I for "the adoption, to wit, the redemption of our body" (Rom. 8:23).

People have said there is no faith in heaven and no hope; they do not know what they say. In heaven faith and hope have their fullest strength and their brightest sphere, for glorified saints believe in God's promise and hope for the resurrection of the body. The apostle tells us that "they without us should not be made perfect" (Heb. 11:40); that is, until our bodies are raised, theirs cannot be raised; until we get our adoption day, neither can they get theirs. "The Spirit and the bride say, Come" (Rev. 22:17). Not only the bride on earth, but also the bride in heaven says, "Come," telling the happy day to hurry, the day when "the trumpet shall sound, and the dead shall be raised incorruptible, and we shall be changed" (1 Cor. 15:52). For it is true, beloved, the bodies that have decayed will rise again; the fabric that has been destroyed by the worm will suddenly form a nobler being; and you and I, though the worm may devour our bodies, will in our flesh behold our God (Job 19:26).

> These eyes shall see him in that day,
> The God that died for me;
> And all my rising bones shall say,
> "Lord, who is like to thee?"

Thus, we desire that our entire manhood, in its trinity of spirit, soul, and body, may be set free from the last vestige of the Fall. We long to put off corruption, weakness, and dishonor, and to wrap ourselves in incorruption, in immortality, in glory, in the spiritual body that the Lord Jesus Christ will bestow on all His people. (See 1 Corinthians 15:42–44.) You can understand in this sense why we groan, for if this body, though redeemed, is really still a captive, and if it is to be completely free and rise to amazing glory one day, those who believe in this precious doctrine may very well groan after it as they wait for it.

Our Public Adoption

There is another point in which the saint is deficient right now, namely, in the manifestation of our adoption. Observe, the text speaks of waiting for the adoption; and another text, further back, explains what that means: "wait[ing] for the manifestation of the sons of God" (Rom. 8:19). In this world, saints are God's children, but you cannot see that they are, except by certain moral characteristics. That man is God's child, a prince of the royal blood, but he wears a workman's clothes. That woman is one of the daughters of the King, but see how pale she is; what wrinkles are on her brow! Many of the daughters of pleasure are far more attractive than she! Why is this? The adoption is not yet manifested; the children are not yet openly declared.

Among the Romans a man could have adopted a child, and that child might have been treated as his for a long time; however, there was a second adoption in public. The child was brought before the authorities and the public, his ordinary garments were taken off, and the adoptive father put on him garments suitable to his new station in life.

"Beloved, now are we the sons of God, and it doth not yet appear what we shall be" (1 John 3:2). We do not yet have the royal robes that distinguish the princes of the blood; we are wearing in this flesh and blood just what we wore as the sons of Adam. However, we know that when He who is the "firstborn among many brethren" (Rom. 8:29) appears, we will be like Him; that is, God will dress us all as He dresses His eldest son. "We shall be like him; for we shall see him as he is" (1 John 3:2).

Can you not imagine that a child taken from the lowest ranks of society and adopted by a Roman senator, would be saying to himself, "I wish the day were here when I will be publicly revealed as the child of my new father. Then, I will take off these plebeian garments, and I will be robed with garments that become my senatorial rank." He is already happy in what he has received, but for that very reason he groans to get the fullness of what is promised him.

It is the same with us today. We are waiting for the day when we will put on our proper garments and be manifested as the children of God. You are young princes, and you have not yet been crowned. You are young brides, and the marriage day has not yet come. And because of the love your fiancé shows you, you long and sigh for the marriage day. Your very happiness makes you groan; your joy, like a swollen spring, longs to leap up like some Iceland geyser, climbing to the skies. Your joy heaves and groans deep within your spirit because it does not have enough room to express itself to others.

Our Liberty

There is a third thing in which we are deficient, namely, liberty, "the glorious liberty of the children of God" (Rom. 8:21). The whole creation is said to be groaning for its share in that freedom. You and I are also groaning for it.

Beloved, we are free. "If the Son therefore shall make you free, ye shall be free indeed" (John 8:36). But, our liberty is incomplete. When Napoleon was on the island of St. Helena, he was watched by many guards; but after many complaints, he enjoyed comparative liberty and walked alone. Yet, what liberty did he have? Liberty to walk around the rock of St. Helena, nothing more.

You and I are free, but what is our liberty? As for our spirits, they have liberty to soar into the third heaven and sit in the heavenly places with Christ Jesus (Eph. 2:6). But, as for our bodies, we can only roam about this small prison cell of earth, feeling that it is not the place for us. Napoleon had been used to gilded halls and all the pomp and glory of imperial state, and it was hard to be reduced to a handful of servants. Even so, we are kings (Rev. 1:5–6)—we are of the imperial blood—but we do not have our proper state as dignities yet; we do not have our royalties here.

We meet with our brothers and sisters here in their earthen temples; we go to our lowly homes; and we are content, so far as these things go. Still, how can kings be content until they mount their thrones? How can a heavenly one be content until he ascends to heaven? How can a celestial spirit be satisfied until it sees celestial things? How can the heir of God be content until he rests on his Father's bosom and is "filled with all the fulness of God" (Eph. 3:19)?

I want you to now observe that we are linked with the creation. Adam was in liberty, perfect liberty; nothing confined him; paradise was exactly fitted to be his seat. There were no wild beasts to tear him apart, no rough winds to cause him injury, no blighting heat to bring him harm. But, in this present world everything is contrary to us. Evidently, we are foreigners here. Ungodly men prosper well

enough in this world. They root themselves
and spread themselves like "green bay tree[s]"
(Ps. 37:35): it is their native soil. But, the
Christian needs the greenhouse of grace to
keep himself alive at all. Out in the world he is
like some strange, foreign bird, native of a
warm and sunny climate; being let loose here
under our wintry skies, he is ready to perish.

Now, God will one day change our bodies
and make them fit for our souls, and then He
will change this world itself. I must not specu-
late, for I know little about this new world.
However, it is no speculation to say that we
"look for new heavens and a new earth,
wherein dwelleth righteousness" (2 Pet. 3:13),
and that there will come a time when "the
leopard shall lie down with the kid...and the
lion shall eat straw like the ox" (Isa. 11:6–7).

We expect to see this world, which is now
so full of sin that it is a field of blood, turned
into a paradise, a garden of God. We believe
that "the tabernacle of God [will be] with men,
and he will dwell with them" (Rev. 21:3), and
"they shall see his face; and his name shall be
in their foreheads" (Rev. 22:4). We expect to
see the New Jerusalem descend out of heaven
from God (Rev. 3:12). In this very place, where
sin has triumphed, we expect that "grace [will]
much more abound" (Rom. 5:20). Perhaps after those great fires of which Peter speaks

when he says, "The heavens being on fire shall
be dissolved, and the elements shall melt with
fervent heat" (2 Pet. 3:12), the earth will be
renewed and will be more lovely than it was
originally. Perhaps, since matter cannot be
annihilated but will be as immortal as spirit,
this very world will become the place of an
eternal jubilee, from which perpetual hallelu-
jahs will go up to the throne of God. If such is
the bright hope that cheers us, we may well
groan for its realization, crying out,

O long-expected day, begin;
Dawn on these realms of woe and sin.

The Unveiling of Our Glory

I will not elaborate further, except to say
that our glory is not yet revealed, and that is
another subject of sighing. "The glorious
liberty" (Rom. 8:21) may be translated, "The
liberty of glory." Beloved, we are like warriors
fighting for the victory; we do not yet share in
the shout of triumph. Even up in heaven they
do not have their full reward. When a Roman
general came home from war, he entered Rome
secretly; and he stayed, perhaps for a week or
two, among his friends. He went through the
streets, and people whispered, "That is the
general, the valiant one," but he was not

publicly acknowledged. But, on the appointed day, the gates were thrown wide open; and the general, victorious from the wars in Africa or Asia, with his snow-white horses bearing the trophies of his many battles, rode through the streets, which were strewn with roses, while the music sounded; and the multitudes, with glad acclaim, accompanied him to the capitol. That was his triumphant entry.

Those in heaven have, as it were, secretly entered there. They are blessed, but they have not had their public entrance. They are waiting for their Lord to "descend from heaven with a shout, with the voice of the archangel, and with the trump of God" (1 Thess. 4:16). Then their bodies will rise; then the world will be judged; then the righteous will be divided from the wicked (Matt. 13:49). The whole blood-washed host will stream upwards in marvelous procession; the Prince will be at their head, leading captivity captive (Ps. 68:18) for the last time. Wearing their white robes and bearing their palms of victory (Rev. 7:9), the saints will march up to their crowns and to their thrones to reign forever and ever! The believing heart is panting, groaning, and sighing for this consummation.

Now, I think I hear somebody say, "You see these godly people who profess to be so happy and so safe; they still groan, and they must confess it." To which I reply, "Yes, that is quite true, and it would be a great mercy for you if you knew how to groan in the same way. If you were half as happy as a groaning saint, you might be content to groan on forever."

I showed you the difference between a hopeless groan and a hopeful groan. I will show you yet again. Go into that house over there, and listen at that door on the left; there is a deep, hollow, awful groan. Go to the next house, and hear another groan. It seems to be, so far as we can judge, much more painful than the first, and it has the severest anguish in it. How are we to judge between them? We will come again in a few days. As we enter the first house, we see weeping faces, flowing tears, and a coffin. Ah, it was the groan of death! We will go into the next. Ah, what is this? Here is a smiling baby, and a father with a glad face; if you venture to look at the mother, see how her face smiles for joy that a man is born into the world. The family is happy and rejoicing. There is all the difference between the groan of death and the groan of life.

Now, the apostle set the whole matter before us when he said, "The whole creation groaneth"—you know what words come next— "and travaileth" (Rom. 8:22). Your groaning and travailing will result in a blessing of the best kind. We are panting, longing after something greater, better, nobler; and it is coming. It is not the pain of death we feel, but the pain of life. We are thankful to have such a groaning.

One night, just before Christmas, two men who were working very late were groaning in two very different ways. One of them said, "Ah, there's a poor Christmas day in store for me; my house is full of misery." He had been a drunkard and a spender and did not have a penny to bless himself with, and his house had become a little hell. He was groaning at the thought of going home to such a scene of quarreling and distress. Now, the man who worked beside him, as it was getting very late, wished to be at home and therefore groaned. A coworker asked, "What's the matter?" "Oh, I want to get home to my dear wife and children. I have such a happy house; I do not like to be away from it." The other might have said, "Ah, you pretend to be a happy man, and here you are groaning." "Yes," he could say, "and you would be blessed if you had the same thing to groan about that I have."

Similarly, the Christian has a good Father and a blessed, eternal home, and he groans to get to it. Ah, there is more joy even in the groan of a Christian, than in all the mirth, merriment, dancing, and lewdness of the ungodly when their mirth is at its greatest height. We are like the dove that flutters and is weary, but thank God, we have an ark to go to. (See Genesis 8:6, 8–9.) We are like Israel in the wilderness: our feet are sore, but blessed be God, we are on the way to Canaan. We are like Jacob looking at the wagons: the more he looked at the wagons, the more he longed to see Joseph's face. (See Genesis 45:25–28.) Our groaning after Jesus is a blessed groan, for

> 'Tis heaven on earth, 'tis heaven above,
> To see his face, and taste his love.

THE SAINTS' STATE OF MIND

Now I will conclude with what our state of mind is. A Christian's experience is like a rainbow: it is made up of drops of earth's griefs and beams of heaven's bliss. It is a checkered scene, a garment of many colors. A Christian is sometimes in the light and sometimes in the dark. The text says, "We ourselves groan" (Rom. 8:23). I have told you what that groan is; I need not explain it further. But, it is added, "We ourselves groan within ourselves." It is not the hypocrite's groan, who goes mourning everywhere, wanting to make people believe that he is a saint because he is wretched. We groan *within ourselves*. Our sighs are sacred things; these griefs and sighs are too hallowed for us to announce in the streets. We tell our longings to our Lord, and to our Lord alone. We groan within ourselves.

It appears from the text that this groaning is universal among the saints; there are no exceptions. We all feel it to some extent. He who is rich with worldly goods and he who is poor, he who is blessed in health and he who suffers with sickness—we all have some measure of an earnest, inward groaning for the redemption of our bodies.

In our text the apostle said we are "waiting" (Rom. 8:23), by which I understand that we are not to sulk, like Jonah or Elijah, when they said, "Let me die." (See Jonah 4:8; 1 Kings 19:4.) Nor are we to sit still and look for the end of the day because we are tired of work; nor are we to become impatient and wish to escape from our present pains and sufferings. We are to groan after perfection, but we are to wait patiently for it, knowing that what the Lord appoints is best. Waiting implies being ready. We are to stand at the door, expecting the Beloved to open it and take us away to Himself.

In the next verse, Romans 8:24, we are described as hoping. The verse says, "We are saved by hope." The believer continues to hope for the time when death and sin will no longer annoy his body. As his soul has been purified, so will his body be; this will be an answer to his prayer that the Lord would sanctify him wholly—body, soul, and spirit. (See 1 Thessalonians 5:23.)

A PRACTICAL APPLICATION

Now, beloved, I will give you a practical application for this somewhat rambling writing. Here is a test for us all. You may judge a man by what he groans after. Some men groan after wealth; they worship money. Some groan continually under the troubles of life; they are merely impatient—there is no virtue in that. Some men groan because of their great losses or sufferings; well, this may be nothing but a rebellious complaining under God's rod, and if so, no blessing will come of it.

But, the man who yearns after more holiness, the man who sighs after God, the man who groans after perfection, the man who is discontented with his sinful self, the man who feels he cannot be at rest until he is made like Christ—he is the man who is blessed indeed. May God help us to groan all our days with that kind of groaning. As I have said before, there is heaven in this groaning, and though the word denotes sorrow, there is a depth of joy concealed within.

> Lord, let me weep for nought but sin,
>   And after none but thee;
> And then I would, O that I might,
>   A constant weeper be.

I do not know a more beautiful sight on earth than a man who has served his Lord many years and who, having grown gray in service, feels that he will soon be called home. He is rejoicing in the firstfruits of the Spirit (Rom. 8:23) that he has obtained, but he is panting after the full harvest of the Spirit that is guaranteed to him. I see him sitting on a jutting crag by the edge of Jordan, listening to the harpers on the other side and waiting until

> *The pitcher [shall] be broken at the fountain, or the wheel broken at the cistern...and the spirit shall return unto God who gave it.*   *(Eccl. 12:6–7)*

A wife waiting for her husband's footsteps, a child waiting in the dark until his mother comes to give him a goodnight kiss—these are portraits of our waiting. It is a pleasant and precious thing to experience this waiting and hoping.

I fear for some of you that have never come and put your trust in Christ. When your time comes to die, you will have to say what Wolsey said, with only one word of alteration:

O Cromwell, Cromwell!
Had I but served my God with half the zeal
I served the world, he would not, in mine age,
Have left me naked to mine enemies.

Oh, before your day to die comes, quit serving the master who can never reward you except with death! Throw your arms around the cross of Christ, and give up your heart to God. Then, come what may,

I am persuaded, that neither death, nor life, nor angels, nor principalities, nor powers, nor things present, nor things to come, nor height, nor depth, nor any other creature, shall be able to separate us from the love of God, which is in Christ Jesus our Lord. (Rom. 8:38–39)

Although you will sigh for a while for more of heaven, you will soon come to the home of blessedness, where "sorrow and sighing shall flee away" (Isa. 35:10).

May the Lord bless you for Christ's sake. Amen.